SOLDIER BOY

SOLDIER BOY

A CHRONICLE OF LIFE AND DEATH AND SURVIVAL DURING WORLD WAR II

George K. Zak

VANTAGE PRESS
New York

Published by Vantage Press, Inc.
516 West 34th Street, New York, New York 10001

Manufactured in the United States of America
ISBN: 0-533-12635-5

Library of Congress Catalog Card No.: 97-91324

0 9 8 7 6 5 4 3 2

For my beloved wife, Joan McAndrew Zak

For our children and grandchildren

and

For all my fellow soldier boys

Contents

Introduction   ix

An Invitation and a Draft   1
Basic Training at Fort Benning, Georgia   4
On to the 106th Infantry Division, Camp Atterbury   9
Heading for Europe   20
A Month in England   22
France and Belgium   24
On the Front Line in Germany   26
The Germans Launch a Gigantic Attack!   29
Abandoning the Schnee Eifel Ridge   32
Attack Schonberg!   35
Surrender!   38
The Boxcars   42
Stalag IV-B at Muhlberg, Germany   46
Dresden and the Blanket Factory at Lobau   67
The Quarry near Hohnstein   76
Dresden Again and Back to Stalag IV-B at Muhlberg   79
The Russians Arrive at Stalag IV-B   86
With the Russians and American Army Reps at Riesa   89
Two Brothers Meet near Oschatz, Germany   98
Back in the U.S. Army   104
The S.S. *Excelsior* and Home   108

Epilogue   111

Introduction

It was 5:30 A.M. on December 16, 1944 and I was jolted awake by the roar of powerful German artillery shells exploding to our rear on American artillery positions and on other rear area targets. German shells were also exploding on other infantry units somewhere to the south of us. I had been sleeping peacefully in our little log and dirt-covered dugout not far from our machine-gun nest and had awakened to a nightmare.

Soon our own artillery started firing back, over our heads. All day long we stood in the bitter cold and snow in the middle of this enormous artillery duel, expecting German tanks and troops to start coming at us from the wooded ridge to the southeast.

I was nineteen years old and a private first class in the American 106th Infantry Division. Our 14,000-man division had recently arrived at what had been a quiet area in the Ardennes Forest just inside Germany, and were thinly spread over a fifteen-mile front. I didn't know it then, but I had a front-row seat at the beginning of the Battle of the Bulge, the biggest battle ever fought by the U.S. Army.

Like everyone else, I was apprehensive, to say the least, and wondered how I managed to be here, of all the places the army could have sent me. I was willing to do my part to help defeat Germany, but being an ammo bearer in a machine-gun squad in the infantry wouldn't have been my first choice. Only 10 percent of the men in service were in the infantry, but the infantry suffered 70 percent of the casualties.

So here I was, Private First Class George Zak, about to meet the enemy and my fate. I hoped I would do my duty, follow my orders, and survive.

•

SOLDIER BOY

An Invitation and a Draft

This story really begins in 1943. I was a senior at St. Patrick Academy, an all-boys high school in Chicago. It was a long commute from my home in suburban Forest Park.

A month or two before graduation, we were all given a test by military officers to see who could qualify for the Army or the Navy Specialized Training Program. The army program was known as the A.S.T.P. At the time of the test I had indicated I preferred the army. The A.S.T.P. was a program designed to keep highly-qualified students in college to provide an ongoing stream of future officers, engineers, linguists, administrators, and so forth.

I was pleased and proud when I later received a letter from the U.S. Army advising me that I had passed the test. The letter went on to say that I would be doing a service to my country and would also be advancing my own military career by joining this program. If I accepted I would enlist in the army reserve and be sent to college until I was eighteen. After I became eighteen years of age I would be transferred to active military service. Then, after taking infantry basic training for three or four months I would return to college in uniform.

I soon realized, however, that because of the way the schedule worked out I would only be in college for three months before I would be transferred to active military service. Going away to college would have involved some expense for clothing, luggage, and so forth, and that would have been a problem.

1

After thinking it over, I decided that I would wait to be drafted and see what happened then. I kept the special card showing that I was eligible for the A.S.T.P., which I was to present when I entered active military service.

So after attending Quigley Preparatory Seminary for three years and my final high school year at St. Patrick Academy, I worked for a while loading and unloading trucks at a Chicago warehouse. Then I went to work for the U.S. Treasury Department at the Merchandise Mart in Chicago. I worked on the night shift, using I.B.M. equipment, sorting in either alphabetical or numerical order punched-hole tab cards representing purchased U.S. Savings Bonds.

I registered for the draft on my eighteenth birthday in September 1943, and received my draft notice in November. Later that month immediately after passing my pre-induction physical, my papers were stamped "NAVY." I made a fateful decision. Knowing the army wanted me for the Army Specialized Training Program, I told them I wanted the army, not the navy. And I never told them why. Very dumb.

As I later realized, I probably would have been put in the Navy Specialized Training Program, and my military service would have been vastly different than the way it actually turned out. At any rate, after my being interviewed by a panel of officers and sergeants, they crossed out "NAVY" and stamped my papers "ARMY."

Several pretty young women, older and more mature than I was, handled some of the clerical work at the processing center. I was still shy around young women and was in awe of their beauty and charm. Just then one of them smiled and winked at me and said, "Come back in two years." I was flustered and a little tongue-tied, but pleased she thought I would be a good prospect down the road. And I certainly hoped that even if I wasn't back THERE in two years, I would at least be SOMEWHERE in two years, alive and kicking. It was a good thing I

2

didn't know then how bleak my chances were for making this happen.

On December 19, 1943, I reported for active duty at Fort Sheridan, Illinois. The first few days were exciting and a little scary as we were given uniforms, more tests, and shown the first of several clinical, gross movies about venereal diseases. So that's what those "fallen women" were all about! These movies were known as "Mickey Mouse" movies. And we heard that women in the Women's Army Corps, known as the WACs, got to see "Minnie Mouse" movies. It was quite a shock for a young man who had been raised in a very protected, some-what puritanical Catholic home. This was just the beginning of my education in the big, rough world I had just entered.

Basic Training at Fort Benning, Georgia

After about two weeks, I found myself on a train full of other guys like myself, all members of the A.S.T.P., heading south. After a long and tedious ride, we arrived at the Infantry Training Center at Fort Benning, Georgia. My brilliant army career was about to begin.

It began with still more tests to make sure we were qualified for the college program, and then, in early January 1944, we started our infantry training. Thousands of young men like myself began a thirteen-week accelerated training program. At that time the normal infantry basic training lasted seventeen weeks.

In alphabetical order, everyone was assigned to a 15-man squad. Four squads formed a platoon of 60 men, and four platoons formed a company, for a total of 240 men. I was assigned to the Fourth Squad of the Fourth Platoon of the Sixteenth Company of the Fourth Training Regiment.

We were now in the clutches of about two dozen officers and non-coms charged with turning 240 young civilians into 240 trained killers. ("Non-com," an abbreviation for "non-commissioned officer," is a general term for sergeants and corporals.) On the first day we were organized, our training sergeant, Tech Sergeant Boyd, announced with great relish, "You might as well turn your souls over to God, because your bodies belong to me."

We all had just turned eighteen, and while we were all bright, we were still naive and inexperienced in the real world. Some were fairly muscular and confident, and many, like myself, were skinny and unsure of themselves. Our training officers and non-coms were older, cocky, and intimidating. Captain Nicholson was my company commander, Second Lieutenant Wells was my platoon leader, Sergeant Joseph Midkiff was my platoon sergeant, and Corporal Kavanaugh was my squad leader. Sergeant Midkiff was tough, but fair, and I eventually looked up to him as a model, dedicated soldier.

Basic training turned out for me to be a combination of tough physical work, excitement, fear, frustration, new confidence, and pride of accomplishment. I also put on a lot of weight, all muscle. And I made a lot of friends.

The main purpose of the training, of course, was to learn how to kill and avoid being killed. We learned an amazing number of ways to kill. Before our training was over, I was proficient in hitting a target with the M1 rifle, the M1 carbine, the .45-caliber semi-automatic pistol, a light, air-cooled .30-caliber machine gun, and a 60-millimeter mortar. I learned how to attack someone with a hatchet or a knife or bayonet, and mastered some basic tricks of jujitsu. We also learned how to fire rockets at a tank from a bazooka, throw hand grenades, fire grenades from a rifle with a grenade launching attachment, plant land mines, and set booby traps.

Along the way we endured long marches in sweltering heat with full field packs, rifles and steel helmets, and at times we slept in two-man pup tents in the woods. We climbed walls and ran through obstacle courses and faced live machine-gun fire a few feet over our heads on the infiltration course. And we learned how to march and salute and do the manual of arms with the M1 rifle. And spread over a number of weeks, we watched each segment of the "Why We Fight" movie, produced by Frank Capra. The army was trying to change us from ordinary, decent civilians into men who would charge and kill on command.

One morning I woke up in our barracks with a fever. While the rest of the men went out for the day's training, I was given a pass to go to the dispensary on sick call. My fever wasn't high enough to have me sent to the hospital, but I was given an admission slip for the sick bay about two miles away. I walked over and when I presented my admission slip, the non-com told me they had no more cots. If I could get a cot, they would fit me in. Otherwise, I wouldn't be admitted.

If I had had any sense, I would just have lain on the floor and let them do something about it. But by now I was a disciplined soldier used to doing what I was told. I shake my head when I think about it now, but, fever and all, I went back to my empty barracks, got my cot and mattress, and carried them back to sick bay. Three or four days and a bunch of aspirin later, I was back on duty. Someone else brought back my cot and mattress.

One day I was summoned to the orderly room and the first sergeant said, "Zak, you didn't take your shots. Take this form and go to the dispensary." I was shocked. I smelled a rat. I had taken all my shots. There was no way I could have avoided it. We had all been marched over to the dispensary a number of times on a schedule and lined up. I quickly realized that either the company clerk or the first sergeant had lost my record. Apparently he was willing to have me take all the shots a second time just to tidy up his records.

This time I didn't cave in. I was getting smarter. I looked the sergeant in the eye, told him why I couldn't have missed getting my shots, and suggested he just get a blank form and fill it in. He looked at me for a couple of seconds and then told me to get out. I never heard any more about it.

Time marched on, and we continued our infantry basic training. I was pleased that I had developed some muscles and I felt a lot more confident of myself. And we all felt good, knowing that one day this tough ordeal would come to an end. We would soon be off to college to study and mature, and one day become army officers or specialists of some kind.

About six or seven weeks into our training, the War Department announced that the Army Specialized Training Program was being abolished. The War Department had concluded that the army now needed trained infantrymen more than it needed soldiers going to college. We were all shocked and devastated. Our plans for attending college were now down the drain. We were in the infantry for good. Some wanted to transfer to the Air Force as aviation cadets, but transfers were no longer allowed.

Our infantry basic training went on as usual. Our battalion, consisting of 960 basic trainees plus our officers, made a long march to the rifle range under very interesting, simulated combat conditions. The sixty men in my platoon were the rear guard. We had men out on both flanks watching for enemy troops and were attacked by "enemy" soldiers firing machine guns at us with blank ammunition. We formed a skirmish line and rushed the machine guns.

The next thing we knew, several "enemy" planes roared very low overhead in a mock strafing attack. Boy, that was exciting. And, farther along the march, some of the men up ahead encountered an attack with tear gas. We all put on our gas masks and plunged ahead. That evening we arrived at some woods and were ordered to dig slit trenches for ourselves. Slit trenches were supposed to be three feet wide, seven feet long, and at least two feet deep. We were all dead tired, and it was tough. After that, we each fixed ourselves a C-ration supper, and then it was time to pitch our two-man pup tents and collapse for the night.

The next morning we were up at 4:30 A.M. and on our way, and after five more hours of marching, we arrived at the rifle range. We stayed there for two full weeks, living in six-man tents, and spent every day at the range trying to master the M1 rifle. Finally, we fired for the record, and I think everyone in my company qualified.

During the following weeks, we practiced attacking "enemy" positions while firing live rifle ammunition, and practiced firing grenade launchers, anti-tank rockets from a bazooka, and 60-millimeter mortars. Finally, our training was over.

On to the 106th Infantry Division, Camp Atterbury

After some delay we were put on a train heading back up north, and finally arrived about April 1, 1944 at Camp Atterbury, Indiana, the home of the 106th Infantry Division.

As we were arriving, the 14,000-man division was in the process of being stripped of more than half of the seasoned soldiers who had just been through rigorous maneuvers in Tennessee. The division had been brought to the peak of its training and efficiency and was now being raided to fill the army's need for replacements overseas. We newcomers were eventually joined by men from the Air Force who had once been in the infantry and by men from replacement depots.

Our group from Fort Benning was soon sorted out and assigned to open slots all over the division. I was assigned to Company D, a heavy weapons company consisting of about 165 officers and men, headed by a captain, and was part of the First Battalion of the 422nd Regiment. The rest of the battalion consisted of three rifle companies, a cannon company, and an anti-tank company. Each of the three rifle companies had about 190 officers and men. The entire battalion consisted of about 835 officers and men headed by a lieutenant colonel.

Most of my friends were assigned to rifle companies or other units throughout the entire division. I was shocked that very few of the friends I had made in the past three months at Fort Benning would be with me in my new company.

I was assigned as an ammunition bearer in Company D in

an 81-millimeter mortar squad. The mortar consisted of three parts. It had a steel base plate, thirty inches square, on which one end of a five-foot long hollow steel tube or barrel would be attached when being fired, held up by a steel A-shaped bipod. Each of these three parts probably weighed about twenty-five pounds. During training the members of the squad had to take turns carrying these heavy hunks of metal around, as well as a short rifle called a carbine. And during actual practice firing, the rest of the squad had to carry, along with a carbine, the 3-1/4 inch diameter mortar shells in pouches hanging in the front and back of a sleeveless jacket.

After four months of hard training in the army, I was stronger and heavier now, but this was backbreaking work. Why couldn't I have been assigned as a plain rifleman, I wondered, and only have to carry an M1 rifle and ammo belts?

I struggled along like this for a month or so, with occasional rest when assigned to K.P. or guard duty. And then a happy opportunity came along.

One morning at our first formation, Captain Porter announced he wanted volunteers for the motor pool. All the company jeeps and our small 3/4-ton truck had been on extensive maneuvers in Tennessee and were in bad shape. They had to be reconditioned. This would be a temporary assignment for about a month. I jumped at the chance. My only problem was that I didn't really know how to drive. I never had access to a car, never had a license, and had only managed to get behind the wheel of a car twice, and only for a few minutes.

Quite a few of us stepped forward, and the motor sergeant went from man to man to pick out the ones he wanted. When he got to me, he asked me how much driving experience I had. I told him, "I drove every chance I got." I was one of those picked.

We were marched right over to the motor pool, a large parking lot loaded with jeeps and trucks. Unlike a rifle company, which had maybe five jeeps, our heavy weapons company rated nineteen jeeps and a 3/4-ton mechanic's truck. We also had fourteen two-wheel trailers for the jeeps.

Lucky for me we didn't have to drive the jeeps at this point. We were assigned jeeps, at first two men to each jeep, and we went to work under the mechanic's supervision. We gradually disassembled, sandpapered, and painted all the removable parts, such as the generator, the starter, and so forth. Later, we helped when the jeep bodies were sprayed with a new coat of olive drab paint.

There was plenty of time to loaf, and while some read comic books while lying hidden from view under the jeep, I practiced shifting gears and getting the general hang of it. I fell in love with the jeep, and soon I was tooling around and having a ball. Finally, all the vehicles were in good shape except for some, like mine, which needed new brake shoes. Brake shoes were in short supply.

Many of us were then selected to go to a special two-week driving school to be conducted by the lieutenant in charge of the motor pool. We had lectures and various demonstrations about care and maintenance and when and how to shift to four-wheel drive and low-low gear. I enjoyed it and learned a lot. We also had a few turns at the wheel of 3/4-ton and 2-1/2-ton trucks. Then we would go on long convoys on back roads in our jeeps. Once we were driving, with both the windshield and the top down, and a hailstorm came up. None of the drivers had goggles, we could not stop, and we had to endure hail hitting us in the eyes as we drove. It was very painful.

One sunny day I was driving my jeep with two fellow students as passengers in a long convoy, and mine was the last jeep in a long line. At times I had to drive like hell to keep up because some guys ahead would fail to maintain the proper interval and then speed up.

I rounded a bend on a dirt road I had never been on,

going as fast as I could trying to catch up, and started down a long, steep hill. To my horror I saw the lieutenant standing on the hood of his jeep at the bottom of the hill, hands on hips, watching "his boys" passing by. His jeep had been parked sideways, blocking the narrow road ahead, and we were expected to make a left turn and proceed over a wooden bridge. Where were my brakes when I needed them?!!

I pumped my brakes as hard as I could, and we were gradually slowing down, but we were still heading for a broadside collision with the lieutenant's jeep. I was sweating bullets and the lieutenant was wide-eyed and frozen with fear. He should have dived off his jeep, but he just stood there paralyzed and bug-eyed.

Just as I got to the bottom of the hill, I swung the wheel hard to the left. The jeep skidded sideways on the dirt road right up to the other jeep, and then shot over the bridge. Why we didn't turn over during that skid, I don't know. What a harrowing experience; none of us could speak for quite a while. I thought I had done a great job but wondered what the lieutenant thought, and whether he had crapped in his pants. He never mentioned it. I suspect he was very embarrassed by his dangerous grandstanding.

But driving school wasn't over yet. A few days later, our convoy was lead along a narrow dirt road and stopped alongside a steep grassy hill on our left, probably fifty or sixty feet high. On the right side of the road stood high bushes and scattered trees. The lieutenant was back in form and announced our final test was to drive our jeeps one at a time up this steep hill all the way to the top, turn around, and come back down.

When it was my turn, I shifted into four-wheel drive and low gear ratio, and with two passengers eased my jeep into the roadside ditch, and then let it claw its way to the top. The good old jeep was quite a machine.

After all the jeeps had a turn, the driver of a 3/4-ton Dodge truck just ahead of us started up the hill. About halfway up the truck ran out of steam and just wasn't capable of coping with a 45-degree hill. The driver eased the truck down while practically standing on the brakes. I had a good view of all this while sitting in my jeep with two buddies right at the base of the hill.

The lieutenant yelled at the driver and told him to "Get that thing up the hill, and this time really pour on the gas." The driver tried again, stalled halfway up, and again had to slowly back down. The lieutenant ordered the hapless driver out of the truck. As the lieutenant got in, he smugly said, "I'll show you how to do it."

He slammed the truck in and out of the ditch and up the hill he went. But he got no farther than the previous driver did. Then the truck started coming backwards down the hill, but it was gaining speed. Maybe he couldn't find the brake pedal. And it was gaining more speed. All of a sudden, the pressure of air whipped up the loose canvas covering the back of the truck, like a sail catching the wind, and draped it over the cab, leaving the lieutenant completely in the dark. The back end of the truck hit the ditch, flew three feet high in the air, and disappeared into the shrubbery across the narrow dirt road.

We sat there with our mouths open, hardly believing what we had just seen. Was he dead, we wondered? Did the truck hit a tree? While we sat there, still stunned by this fantastic "air show," the lieutenant came stumbling out of the shrubbery looking shaken and disheveled, but apparently unhurt. We tried not to laugh, but we silently gave him an "A" for effort.

The day finished without any further comic touches, and school soon came to an end. We were now all licensed army drivers, and I was pleased to be designated as the official driver for my squad. I now "owned" jeep D-19 and its two-wheel trailer.

And that meant that most of the time I was on duty at the motor pool, driving officers or food or equipment around. And

I still wince when I recall the day when another jeep driver pulled alongside and challenged me to a race. We were both pulling empty two-wheel trailers. We got up to fifty and sixty miles per hour, side by side, when I chickened out. I guess this showed I had more sense, but not much more. It's amazing what bad judgment a young man can have.

Everyone pulled guard duty once in a while, and once, instead of walking a beat, I was assigned one Saturday night to the beer hall at the P.X., or Post Exchange. I had to stand just inside the door wearing a plastic helmet and an M.P. armband, holding a wooden police nightstick. The beer flowed freely, and in theory I was to break up any fights that broke out. I was bigger and stronger now than when I first joined the army, but I would have been in big trouble if any fights did break out. And there was no way to get any help. For three hours I sweated bullets while trying to look intimidating. But the gods of war smiled on me that night and no fights broke out on my shift.

Once in a while, we would have a field exercise and I would be back to lugging mortar shells while our own artillery was firing over our heads. In addition to infantry battalions, every infantry division also had four artillery battalions.

Things were finally getting better. Less drudgery and more freedom. And one day I was no longer Private Zak. I had been moved up one notch to the exalted rank of private first class, and got, I think, about a four-dollar raise in monthly pay. And I had good friends like John Wilson, Dave Wyman, Jack Zordell, and Staff Sergeant Charlie Smith, the mess sergeant.

Once we were spending the day on the carbine range, getting more experience. By then most of us were pretty good, and it was boring. All our shooting was in the prone position, and in groups of two, we spent hours taking turns taking one shot at a time at a large target three hundred yards away. After each shot, a soldier in the pits would lower the target below ground level, put a marker on the bullet hole, and raise the target so our marker could be seen. Then the target would be lowered again, the marker would be removed, and the target would be raised again for the next shot. It was very tedious.

My buddy and I decided it was time to make this whole thing more interesting. The two guys to our left were about fifteen feet away, taking turns shooting at the adjoining target. We decided to have some fun.

One of us would take aim at their target, and the other would let him know when the soldier in the adjoining group was starting to squeeze his trigger, aiming at the same target. We would then get off a quick shot at their target and it would start going down an instant before the poor guy could pull the trigger. Once, one of them followed the bull's-eye down with his gun sight until the bull's-eye and the target disappeared below ground level.

Naturally, they became very confused and upset, and finally complained to the sergeant and lieutenant in charge of the firing line. We had a heck of a time not laughing or bringing any attention to ourselves while the lieutenant raged on the phone at the baffled sergeant in charge of the targets.

One day, back at the motor pool, the dispatcher ordered me to pick up a certain lieutenant from another company and drive him to a particular training area several miles away. He was involved in training some soldiers how to fire a mortar.

So I picked him up and I was zipping along this country dirt road going a little faster than I should have. The road turned to the right and then to the left to go around a hill. Just after I made my turn to the right, I saw the grill of a two and a half ton army truck rounding the bend just ahead, heading for us, and he was using most of the road. The driver was as surprised to see us as we were him. I had almost nowhere to go to avoid a collision. To my right was a drainage ditch, and if I went in, we would be killed for sure.

The truck driver kept coming, hugging the side of the hill

on his right. So I leaned my head out the left side of the jeep to guide it as close to the truck as I could without colliding with it. My left ear was practically touching the truck's huge tires as we whizzed past each other. My heart was in my throat and I'm sure the lieutenant had the same reaction.

It took me a while to compose myself and I just kept driving down the road without daring to say anything or even look sideways at the lieutenant. Actually, although I had been driving too fast for the conditions at hand, I was pretty proud of my quick thinking and driving skill. I had thoughtlessly put our lives at risk, and then I saved them. Finally, after we both had our composure back, the lieutenant said something like "Do you always drive like this?" I mumbled, "No, sir," and drove the rest of the way very chastened and embarrassed. I finally realized that driving was a serious responsibility, both for my sake and the sake of others. If I kept this up, I would be killed long before I ever got to any battlefield.

The people of nearby Indianapolis were very used to seeing the officers and men of the 106th Infantry Division on the street or in bars or restaurants, and they always treated us well. Practically everybody had friends and relatives in service somewhere, and I guess we came to represent them in some way.

On July 4, 1944, the 106th Infantry Division put on a massive, impressive, patriotic parade for the good citizens of Indianapolis. It was a beautiful summer day, and it seemed half the people of Indianapolis and other nearby towns lined the sidewalks, many cheering and waving flags.

The crowd watched enthralled as endless rows of riflemen marched by, led by various marching bands and many American flags. All our trucks and towed artillery pieces rolled by, and we jeep drivers passed four abreast. The town loved it, and we all felt very proud.

One evening we arrived at the infiltration course to go

through it in darkness. This would be more scary than in day-time. Machine guns had been set up on a platform, facing a long trench about fifty yards away. A large group of us would enter the trench, and then on signal crawl out of the trench and crawl toward the machine guns, holding our rifles by one hand near the muzzle.

The machine guns would then start firing about five or six feet above our heads. Every fifth round was a tracer bullet and made a continuous red streak as the bullets whizzed by. We had to crawl until we reached another trench just in front of the machine guns. Like it or not, we had to go.

As we got off the trucks, we found ourselves standing next to the body of a soldier who had just been killed. His body had been moved to the side of the road and an army ambulance was just pulling up. We guessed he had panicked and stood up. He lay on his back and they had just taken off his helmet. The top of his head was a bloody mess. When they put down his helmet, I could see it had a bullet hole in front, and the inside was filled with blood and brain tissue.

To my horror I recognized him as the soldier in charge of the grease rack at the motor pool. The next thing I knew, it was our turn and I was scared to death. But out of the trench we came, and all made it safely to the next trench.

By this time men had stopped being shipped out as over-seas replacements, and all the non-coms who had been shipped out had been replaced. The trouble was, as far as we former A.S.T.P. guys were concerned, that most of the replace-ment non-coms were guys who had returned from the Air Force. Many of them had earned corporal or sergeant stripes in the Air Force and were therefore put in charge. We were smarter, but they were luckier. The Air Force was now in charge of the infantry, or so it seemed to us. We were doomed to be privates or privates first class forever.

My gloom disappeared when I got word one day that a

number of us were getting furloughs home for ten days or so. This would be my second one. I also had a furlough not long after I had finished basic training back at Fort Benning, Georgia. I soon arrived at Chicago's Union Station, tanned and fit, and I was sure I cut an impressive figure with my uniform and the stripes of a private first class and my sharpshooter and marksman badges. And I had put on weight and muscle, and now weighed 155 pounds. I had a wonderful time seeing my family and any friends who happened to be home on furlough, and celebrated my nineteenth birthday. But I had this uneasy feeling that our training was about over and that we would soon be heading somewhere overseas.

When I reported back to Company D at Camp Atterbury, Indiana, I was dismayed to find out that some of us were being transferred to other units. It was September 1944. In my case I was transferred to Company M, the heavy weapons company of the Third Battalion, 422nd Regiment, and assigned to a .30-caliber, water-cooled, machine-gun squad in the Third Platoon. And worse, the squad already had a jeep driver, so I became assistant driver. That meant I would only get to drive if something happened to the regular driver.

After my transfer I seldom saw the friends I had made in my old company and had to start all over. In due time I became good friends with a guy in my new squad, Private First Class Leonard Golardi.

Captain James Perkins was company commander of my new company, Company M, and First Lieutenant Jack Stein was the executive officer. I no longer remember the names of any of the other officers. I do remember tough, gruff Ted Straub was first sergeant. For some reason I no longer remember my squad sergeant's name, but I do remember he was an older regular army man. Others I remember include Tech Sergeants Jim Melton and John Taylor, Staff Sergeants Laverne

Borrison, Bob King, and Vince Buckley, Sergeants Bill Finn and Grady Wise, and Privates First Class Jack Zordell, Jim Blair, Herb Meagher, and Maynard Adolphson.

Heading for Europe

After many rumors we finally got our orders to move from Camp Atterbury, Indiana, and on October 13, 1944, the entire division went by train to Camp Myles Standish, near Boston. After a relatively short time, we entrained for New York and went directly by small boats across to the docks in New Jersey.

There, the 422nd and the 424th Regiments boarded an enormous, 901 foot-long, 31-year-old, four-stack Cunard liner, the *Aquitania,* on the evening of October 20. I later read that in its heyday it was a favorite with the Hollywood set, royalty, government officials, famous athletes, and other luminaries. We were about to cross the Atlantic Ocean. (Our other regiment, the 423rd, crossed the Atlantic on the *Queen Elizabeth,* and some units crossed on the *Wakefield.*)

However, the *Aquitania* was now a troop carrier, and probably at least 8,000 of us were shoehorned into five-high bunks. On the following morning, October 21, we sailed, unescorted, toward an unknown destination.

I was lucky. Our company was assigned to bunks on "B" Deck, in what had once been a ballroom. High ornate ceilings and easy access to fresh air right outside the door. Many of the troops were below the water line, all the way down to "G" deck, where they had to endure the smell of engine fuel as well as body odors. Most of us had queasy stomachs much of the way, and didn't venture down to the mess hall on "D" Deck too often. The mess hall smelled of rotten eggs and our latrines smelled of vomit.

One day, I was leaning idly on a railing on "B" Deck, looking backward at the wake the ship was leaving behind us. Looking to my right, I noticed a small ship on our port side, maybe a half a mile away and somewhat behind us, heading in the same direction. At that moment a group of British sailors appeared on "C" Deck, right below me, and started fussing with one of the big deck guns. Before I realized what they were up to, the deck gun went off with a tremendous roar. My ears were ringing and my teeth almost fell out. When I recovered my senses, I watched the shell splash and explode just beyond the bow of the other ship. By that time the British gun crew had disappeared. The other ship veered away and that was that.

Eight days later, on October 29, 1944, after sailing up the Irish Sea between Ireland and England, we arrived at Greenock, Scotland, by way of the Firth of Clyde. It would be safe to say we were all damn glad to be back on solid ground.

A Month in England

We immediately boarded a train and headed south for England. We all enjoyed seeing the pleasant English countryside along the way. The always exuberant Staff Sergeant Laverne Borrison led our group in slightly-racy songs. The following day, October 30, our company arrived, on foot the last few miles, at a little medieval market town that called itself Stow on the Wold, in the Cotswolds. Our transit camp, just outside town, was a collection of metal Nissen huts, each with a small coal-burning stove.

The weather in November was cold and damp, and our company did light marches and other training to pass the time. I weighed about 155 pounds and was strong and fit. My proudest moment was at the range, where I scored twelve out of fifteen bull's-eyes at 300 yards with my carbine. Everyone nearby was impressed, and I had my fifteen seconds of fame. My platoon sergeant came over and I thought he was going to congratulate me. But he didn't say anything and simply took down the serial number of my carbine.

During this time I had a three-day pass. Along with a buddy, I made a quick trip by various buses to the cities of Stratford-on-Avon, Coventry and Oxford, and to Warwick Castle. In an almost-empty modern theatre in Stratford, we saw a stage production of the play *Ten Little Indians,* also known as *And Then There Were None.*

At the city of Coventry, we made our way on foot for several miles past bombed-out, gutted homes and other buildings, and finally arrived at what was left of ancient Coventry

Cathedral. The city had been fire-bombed in late 1940 by the German air force at the beginning of what came to be known as "the Blitz," and everyone had heard about the destruction of this venerable cathedral. My buddy and I made our way in stunned silence through piles of stones and blackened timbers. The walls were more or less still standing, but the entire roof was gone. I returned to my camp at Stow on the Wold in a sad, reflective mood.

About two weeks later, we were issued a basic supply of ammunition for our carbines or pistols, and for our eight machine guns and six mortars. We were ready to be committed to battle. Then we, the 165 officers and men of Company M of the Third Battalion of the 422nd Regiment of the 106th Infantry Division, began our trip to France and whatever lay beyond.

France and Belgium

Most of our men boarded the S.S. *Monowai* at Liverpool on December 2, 1944 and arrived at Le Havre, France, on December 6 after marking time in the Le Havre estuary during some bad weather.

In my case, our group drove our regiment's jeeps and trucks to Southampton, loaded all our vehicles on three LSTs, and left for France on November 29.

After marking time for three days in the English Channel, we sailed up the Seine River. All around us we could see the devastation left in the wake of the Normandy invasion about five months before. Burned-out tanks, sunken boats, shell holes, ruined buildings. I know we were all thinking about what might lie in store for us. Little did we know. We finally drove our vehicles on to a dock at Rouen, the town where Joan of Arc had been burned at the stake during a much earlier war. It was December 1, 1944, and we were in France.

After about an hour's drive, we all ended up in the middle of a large muddy field and pitched our little two-man pup tents. By now winter had really arrived and we all suffered in the cold and wind and dampness. I would have given anything for one of those wool-knit face masks.

Our combat boots were not waterproof, and we all walked around with cold, wet feet. Our barracks bags did not catch up to us for several days, and I did not have a spare, dry pair of socks. One day, spotting a little bonfire up against a fallen log, I saw my chance to dry out my socks. While perched on the log, I took off my boots and held my damp socks over the flame to dry them out. Before I knew it, the toes of the socks caught fire. I put out the fire, put my toeless socks back on, and trudged back in the mud.

After about a week, our company left in a convoy of jeeps and trucks, heading for the front. We arrived in the Ardennes area on the evening of December 7 in the bitter cold. Jim Blair, the driver, I, as assistant driver, and our corporal slept in our jeep that night. We all slept soundly and woke in the morning covered in deep snow. We weren't allowed to have the top or windshield up, but it would not have made any difference. We moved on to the company area and pitched our pup tents in deep snow.

On the Front Line in Germany

On December 9, we moved out in a convoy heading east and entered the town of St. Vith, Belgium. Our officers gave us orders to load our rifles or carbines and be on the alert for possible snipers. We were near the front and the German border and anything could happen. There was no visible sign of war damage in St. Vith, at least that I noticed.

Our convoy was inching along, with many delays. All the while we could hear our own artillery firing and could see muzzle flashes to the southeast of St. Vith. I now knew for sure that we were about to be committed at this front, and hoped to God our officers and their commanders knew what they were doing.

When our jeep got close to the east end of St. Vith, we could now see what the delay was. A German artillery piece was zeroed in on the crossroads, and was lobbing in shells in an erratic pattern. An MP was in charge, and as soon as the shelling stopped, he would jump out of a foxhole and wave a group of vehicles ahead. Then he would call a stop and jump back in his foxhole to wait out the next barrage.

As our jeep inched forward waiting our turn, we stared at the body of a dead American soldier lying face down in the ditch, his arms and legs spread apart. He had been carried there earlier after being killed by an artillery shell. It was the first time I saw a dead American soldier except for one killed by accident by a machine-gun bullet on our infiltration course back at Camp Atterbury, Indiana. It was a sad, sobering moment.

When we got our signal to go, Jim Blair poured on the coal because we soon found ourselves heading south on an open road, and for all we knew, the German artillery had this road zeroed in as well. To our left was a long north-south ridge, which we later learned was the Schnee Eifel, or Snow Mountain. We eventually made our way east up to the top of the Schnee Eifel and turned a little north. Here my corporal and I were dropped off where our company began to assemble. That was the last time I saw Jim Blair or our jeep. The entire ridge was a thick forest of evergreen trees, and our positions were several miles inside Germany.

We then met GI's from the Second Infantry Division, a battle-hardened outfit that was pulling out. This area had been captured in September by another outfit, the Fourth Infantry Division. The guys from the Second Infantry Division told us we would have it easy because only patrol action and some artillery shelling had been going on for some time. "It was a good place to get some combat experience."

My squad took over a machine-gun nest left by the Second Division at the top of the ridge looking down the valley to the southeast. The squad, along with several other non-coms, also inherited a below-ground dugout with several chicken-wire bunks. The dugout was covered with heavy logs with layers of sandbags piled on top. A small opening had been left at the back for an entrance, protected by a low log fence. We took turns using it, fully clothed, with our loaded carbines at our side, when it wasn't our turn in the machine-gun nest, two hours on and four hours off, around the clock, day after day.

There was no real way to wash or keep clean. But our squad did have its own luxury "latrine." It was a designated spot of ground about thirty yards to the rear of our dugout. And a discarded German helmet was available if we wanted to dig a little hole. One of the sergeants made it clear that good sanitation was vital, and anyone caught relieving himself anywhere else would be in big trouble. That was fair enough.

In the valley to our front, we could see rows of four-foot-high concrete dragon's teeth tank obstacles running northeast to southwest, and we could see another ridge on the other side of the valley held by the Germans. This was part of the old Siegfried Line. Not far to the left of our machine-gun nest was an abandoned concrete pillbox.

Our company was thinly spread out along the top of the ridge, and the next gun position both to the left and right was well out of earshot. It bothered me that when I was in the machine-gun nest with a buddy, we were the entire American front line at that point. I found out after the war that our division had to cover a fifteen-mile front, not counting a seven-mile front covered by the Fourteenth Cavalry Group attached to our division.

From December 9, when Company M arrived, through December 15, we settled into our routine: two hours in the machine-gun nest, staring out at the dragon's teeth and the ridge beyond, then four hours for sleep or getting a meal. Our orders at this point were to fire our machine guns only with approval from battalion headquarters. During this period patrols were sent out each night, and during the day, the 589th Field Artillery Battalion, to our rear, was sending occasional volleys of shells whistling over our heads toward the German lines. I don't recall any response during this period from the German artillery.

On December 15, we began to hear from across the valley, from the woods covering the ridge, the sound of trucks or other vehicles grinding their gears and straining their engines while moving over steep ground. And once I saw a thin column of smoke rising. I know our sergeants reported this to company headquarters, but we heard nothing further about it.

The Germans Launch a Gigantic Attack!

At 5:30 A.M. on December 16, 1944, I was jolted awake by the roar of powerful German artillery shells exploding to our rear on American artillery positions and on other rear area targets. German shells were also exploding on other infantry units somewhere to the south of us. I had been sleeping peacefully in our little log and dirt-covered dugout not far from our machine gun nest and had awakened to a nightmare.

Soon our own artillery started firing back, over our heads. All day long we stood in the bitter cold and snow in the middle of this enormous artillery duel, all the while expecting German tanks and troops to start coming at us from the wooded ridge to the southeast.

Suddenly, we saw the first of many V-1 rockets, known as "buzz bombs," passing overhead from somewhere behind the ridge to the east. We had heard about them falling on London but never expected to see them here. They seemed to be passing only about three or four hundred feet above us, gaining altitude, and going just fast enough to stay in the air. They sounded like a freight train rumbling by, and the ground trembled. I estimated they were launched just behind the front at a low trajectory and were still gaining speed.

The V-1's kept coming all day, and all night, and were apparently headed for targets far to the rear. They were also called "flying gas mains" because they looked like a big, wide twenty-five-foot-long pipe with short, stubby wings on the sides and with a large flame shooting out the rear from a second, smaller pipe suspended on top. We watched and worried.

They were bad enough to watch during the day, but at night they were really terrifying. There was snow all over the ground and, when one passed over, the large flame shooting out the rear would light up our faces and the ground with an eerie, spooky, flickering orange light. We would hold our breath and hope it would keep going. The V-1's were filled with a certain amount of fuel, and when the fuel ran out, the motor would quit and the V-1 would fall and explode.

No V-1's ever fell on our positions. In fact, no German artillery hit us either. For the time being, we had box seats at a fantastic show from hell, and we never knew what the next act would be. We were all scared and anxious. I remember I hoped I would survive without being cowardly.

During the afternoon of the 16th, both German and American rifles and automatic weapons were firing on and off both to our left and our right. The German Schmeisser machine pistol had a distinctive sound, the bullets swishing out very fast, like water out of a hose. A lot of our own Browning automatic rifles, or B.A.R.s, were firing on our left. And a rifle bullet fired from the east hit a log just above and to the right of my head while I was at our machine gun. I couldn't figure out what they could have been aiming at. It may have been just a stray shot.

On December 17, we were told that German paratroopers had landed in our rear. They were being routed and we should expect to find them trying to get back east through our positions. We then took our machine gun out of the nest facing east and set it up on the ground facing to our rear. No paratroopers ever materialized.

From then on our squad posted two sentries on two-hour shifts around the clock to watch for any Germans coming from our rear. In the middle of one dark night, I was one of the guys on sentry duty, staring into the dark woods behind our dugout. After standing around for a while, I decided to squat with my back against a two-foot-high wall at the back of the dugout, with my carbine across my knees. It was very quiet, and very dark.

Suddenly I became aware of a warm, smelly liquid hitting the back of my neck, and spraying down on the glove on my right hand and on my carbine. I jumped up, whirled around, and found myself staring into the face of the sergeant who had warned everyone about the dire consequences of not using the open-air latrine away from the dugout.

I was outraged, and he was shocked and humiliated. He implored me not to tell anyone, because he realized if I did, he would be the laughing stock of our entire company. I promised I would not tell anyone, and I never did. But this messy incident reminded me that in the army in those days, if a guy didn't get a promotion he thought he deserved, he would often say he was "p—d on and passed over." Since I hadn't received a promotion in quite a while, I guess I was living proof of this bit of army wisdom.

The next day our artillery was firing fewer and fewer shells, and finally stopped altogether. We continued our two-hours on, four-hours off routine, around the clock. We didn't know it at the time, but we men of the 422nd and 423rd Regiments were almost completely cut off from the rear. And our artillery to our rear was trying to escape being overwhelmed by German troops. But rumors abounded that the Fourteenth Cavalry Group was successfully repulsing the Germans to our north at the Losheim Gap. I learned after the war that just the opposite was the truth.

Abandoning the Schnee Eifel Ridge

About 10:00 A.M. on December 18, I had breakfast in our open-air kitchen, the menu including some pancakes. I didn't know it then, but it was to be my last square meal for five months.

When I got back to our little below-ground dugout, I was told we were pulling out at 10:30 A.M. Before we left we put our duffel bags containing extra clothes and personal effects, such as letters from home I received in England, in one of the below-ground dugouts. One of our lieutenants told a sergeant to place a booby-trap explosive at the entrance, but the sergeant flat out refused to do so. And that was that. I admired him for rejecting an unwarranted order. I was ready to kill Germans, but not that way.

And so Company M, including Private First Class George Zak and about 165 others started out along with the rest of the 422nd Regiment on what proved to be a very tough march.

I was wearing combat boots, a pair of recently acquired rubber overshoes, a new pair of wool socks, underwear, olive drab wool shirt and pants, a wool sweater, a fingertip-length thinly-lined field jacket, a wool scarf, a wool overcoat, a wool knit cap, wool gloves, and my steel helmet and its attached plastic helmet liner.

I had my full field pack strapped on my back containing a pouch for extra socks and underwear, toiletries, some K-Rations, a large can of hot dogs I got on the LST, a rubber raincoat, a rolled-up sleeping bag, and a steel hatchet with a wooden handle. My six-pound carbine was slung over one shoulder, my gas mask in its carrying case was slung over the other, and four hand grenades were in my overcoat pockets.

Around my waist I wore a web belt from which hung canvas pouches containing three or four fifteen-round magazines for my carbine, an eight-inch dagger called a trench knife, in its scabbard, a metal canteen filled with water, a first-aid kit containing a packet of sulfa powder and a large bandage, a bubble sight to attach to the stock of my carbine for launching hand grenades, and a metal sleeve to attach to the muzzle of the carbine to hold a hand grenade in a special launching bracket. And in each hand, I carried a steel box filled with belts of .30-caliber ammunition for our machine gun. Others in our squad carried our machine gun and its tripod, a spare barrel, or more ammunition boxes. We were all moving warehouses.

I wasn't a very big guy, and like most of the others, I started to feel the strain as we made our way through the mud and snow in an unfamiliar forest, feeling like an overloaded pack animal. At one point we hiked up a long winding trail and I began to see discarded overcoats, ammunition boxes, and other equipment along the way.

Hours later, as I felt hot and flushed, I threw away my gas mask and its carrying case. Later, I threw away my hand grenades. I was getting desperate. And sometime later, which I lived to bitterly regret, I took off my wool overcoat and threw it aside. Now I was down to my fingertip-length lined field jacket. But I did hang onto those vital ammunition boxes.

We seemed to be wandering somewhat aimlessly and would rest whenever the column stopped. We marched along most of the day, back into Belgium, but as it turned out, our final destination was only several miles away. Some time during the day, we were told we were going to attack the Belgian town of Schonberg and recapture it from the Germans. Then we would cross a river and set up defensive positions. At dusk our company set up our machine guns, and probably our mortars, and then dug slit trenches for ourselves. Up to this point, we had not run into any Germans. Just as we were falling asleep, we were told to get up. We were moving out.

Like others, I fell down several times when I tripped over something and fell in the mud in the inky darkness. The first time, my steel helmet and liner went flying somewhere, never to be seen again. We were in a rush, and I couldn't stop to make a search in the fog and darkness. Later, in the dark, I again tripped on a root or something, and tumbled down a ravine we were crossing. This time my sleeping bag broke loose and unrolled, and I had to drop it in order to manage my carbine and two steel chests. My rubber raincoat also disappeared somewhere in the mud and fog.

We walked until everyone was exhausted. Finally, Company M halted in an open field near a road. We did not set up any kind of defensive positions except for guards on lookout and were told we would stay there till morning. I had to stand guard for the first hour, which was just fine because I kept warmer walking around then lying in the mud. When my hour was up, I just stood around the rest of the dark night, like many others, and got no sleep whatever. All night long we watched those V-1 rockets grinding along through the air above us, and we could see lights and flashes of explosions from artillery off in the distance.

Attack Schonberg!

As dawn broke on the morning of December 19, our company resumed our march, heading for our attack on Schonberg. As we trudged along, Staff Sergeant Borrison called out, "Guys, it's beer tonight in Schonberg!" I'm not sure he or anyone else believed it, but it was a nice thought.

Still cold, exhausted, hungry, and scared, Company M, along with other troops, arrived at the top of a slope looking down at the little town of Schonberg. At the bottom of the slope, we could see houses or barns and a church steeple just beyond. We could see no exposed enemy gun positions or troops, but we knew the Germans were there in force, watching us. They would have plenty of artillery; we had none.

Apparently, because our battalion and regimental commanders were not sure just what they were going to do, and when, we just milled around wondering what would come next. I remember watching our company commander, Captain James Perkins, sitting on a small rise in the ground talking quietly and grimly with several other officers. He, too, was waiting and wondering.

For my part I wasn't anxious to start the attack, but I knew that the longer we waited the better prepared the Germans would be. I could imagine them piling up huge piles of artillery and mortar shells, along with wagon loads of machine gun and rifle ammunition. I wondered why we didn't advance on the town at first light, without delay. To pass the time, and get a little energy, I cut open the can of hot dogs I had been carrying, and shared them, one each, with the members of my squad.

After what seemed like several hours, we finally got the order to spread out and advance down the long slope leading to Schonberg. Immediately, the Germans opened up on us with artillery and mortar shells, and sprays of machine-gun fire. Explosions were everywhere. Not a single German gun or soldier could be seen. I stumbled ahead with my carbine slung over my shoulder and a heavy steel box in each hand. Our squad machine gun wasn't firing. It was just being carried forward until a suitable target could be identified. We couldn't waste our limited supply of ammunition. Once we opened up, we would run out of ammo in just a few minutes. We moved ahead, waiting to be mowed down by machine-gun fire or blown apart by an artillery or mortar shell. The mortar shells could be seen coming in a high arc while turning end for end, and then, blam!

Men were falling, and the rest of us finally stopped advancing. I felt like a target in a shooting gallery. Out in the open, with no one to shoot at, waiting to be killed. Finally, the order was given to go back up to the top of the slope. Our attack had fizzled. We then made our way to some nearby woods where we would reassemble.

My squad got back together and crouched among the trees, waiting for orders. Just then a lieutenant colonel I didn't recognize came rushing by with a wild look in his eyes. He shouted to us that we wouldn't be talking so loud if we had been under mortar attack as he had just been. That didn't make a lot of sense, but none of us was thinking too clearly.

Our squad then moved farther into the woods and came upon a little clearing. While several squads lay prone on the snow-covered ground, Captain Perkins and my squad sergeant stood in the clearing discussing where to set up our machine gun. Just then a shell exploded among us, probably a mortar shell, and I bounced a few inches off the ground. Then another shell hit, and another, and another. Each time I bounced a little in the air, but was not hit.

The shelling stopped and I immediately heard cries for a medic. Captain Perkins was lying on the ground with one leg just about severed just below the knee. And my buddy Leonard Golardi was lying in the snow, glassy-eyed, with blood oozing from his hip. If others were hit, I didn't see them. Leonard Golardi would later die, but I never found out when or where.

Immediately, one of our sergeants—I think it was First Sergeant Ted Straub—ordered the rest of us to leave the wounded for others to care for, and advance farther into the woods. That was the last I saw of my friend Golardi.

A while later we ran into six of our men carrying Captain Perkins on a stretcher that they had made from two tree branches and an overcoat. I took a turn for a time and could see Perkins was unconscious and had a pale, strained look on his face. I never saw him again. I heard after the war that he finally died and had to be left by the side of a road.

Surrender!

Our company, now under the command of First Lieutenant Jack Stein, helped form a defensive circle of slit trenches in the woods, surrounding a clearing where the wounded were being brought. I soon noticed that our regimental commander, Colonel George L. Descheneaux, had set up his command post next to the wounded men, about a hundred feet from my slit trench.

The rest of the morning, and part of the afternoon, we dug our trenches, watched the wounded being brought in, and wondered what would happen next. The situation was very grim. We didn't have the firepower to break out of our position, we didn't have enough ammunition to fight off a strong attack, and we had no food, water, or adequate medical supplies. Meanwhile, the front had moved to the west of us, and we were now just a large pocket to be mopped up by the Germans.

Later, one of our company officers came by, and passed along the plan that we were going to try to hold out until dark, and then try to slip away in squad groups. After dark we were to go ten miles east, then ten miles north, then start back west to get back to our own lines. Apparently, someone guessed that we would somehow encounter the smallest number of German troops by taking this route. I thought this was a very, very bad idea, heading ten miles into Germany, into the teeth of the dragon. However, nothing ever came of it.

Later still, I looked around and was amazed to see some German soldiers and a German officer standing about fifty feet from me near the colonel and some of the other American officers. One German stayed at the edge of the woods with a machine pistol surveying the scene. Someone was holding a white flag made from several handkerchiefs. I read after the war that Colonel Descheneaux had decided our position was hopeless and saw nothing to gain except slaughter if we continued to fight. He had then sent an officer down the hill with the white flag to try to negotiate a surrender.

A wave of fury swept over me, and I wanted to shoot the German soldiers. After all, these were the men who were killing us. I soon calmed down and realized this was a stupid idea; these men were here under a flag of truce.

I believe it was about 4:00 P.M. when the order was passed that we were surrendering. We were to break up our weapons and wait for the Germans. I got the most sickening, gut-wrenching, helpless feeling. During the year I had served in the army, I sometimes entertained the idea that one day I might get killed or maimed in battle, but never gave any serious thought to the idea of being captured.

So the men, all in a state of shock, started breaking up their weapons. A corporal standing next to me tried to unload his .45 automatic and managed to shoot himself in his right leg. He had removed the clip but made the dumb mistake of leaving the round in the chamber. He apparently only grazed his leg, and limped off to the aid station.

I waited as long as I could to break up my beloved carbine. I had carried it, cleaned it, fired it many times in training, and considered it my friend, my prized possession, and finally, my last defense against a hateful, vicious enemy. I scattered all my rounds in the snow, then disassembled the trigger mechanism as far as I could, and threw the parts into the snow. Then I placed the carbine against a tree and broke the wooden stock with a blow from the bottom of my foot. I was no longer a real soldier, only a trapped rat waiting to be put in a cage. Or waiting to be machine gunned, or sent to a salt mine. We hated their guts, and they hated ours.

German soldiers soon poured into our area and had us all line up to be searched for weapons, watches, and cigarettes. They separated the officers and marched us all down the hill. At the bottom I was shocked to see all the artillery pieces the Germans had lined up facing our positions. We walked long into the night, heading back into Germany, with armed German soldiers walking alongside about every fifty feet.

One scene along the way still remains etched in my memory. Our column of humiliated, despairing prisoners passed through a high wall made of giant tree trunks along a narrow dirt road. On our left we passed rows and rows of barbed-wire fences. On one of the fences, facing ahead, sprawled the body of a dead German soldier. On our right, about a hundred yards ahead, lay the wreckage of an American half-track. Unused belts of .50-caliber machine gun rounds were draped all over the wreckage. And on the ground behind it lay the body of a dead American soldier. I noticed he didn't have any socks or boots. Someone, probably a German, had salvaged those precious items.

Several hours later, as we shuffled along in the dark, I was startled to notice that the man to my right was a young officer wearing an enlisted man's overcoat. I didn't know him, but I could see the crossed rifles emblem of an infantry officer on his shirt collar. I guessed he had grabbed a discarded enlisted man's overcoat to avoid the tight security the Germans had put around the officers. I didn't speak to him, but I kept my eye on him as we walked along.

He was very tense, and his eyes sparkled with adrenaline. A hill came up on our right, and as we began a turn to the right past the hill, out of sight for a few seconds of the guard behind us, the young officer bolted up the hill to try to escape. We all turned to watch, until someone hissed, "Don't look!" We turned our eyes to the front and trudged on, waiting for the sound of gunfire. There was none. I don't know whatever happened to that brave young man, but the odds are he didn't get very far.

That night we slept on the ground at a German town called Prum. Still no food. The next day we marched farther east to the next town, Gerolstein, and were allowed to sleep in a large barn or storehouse. Again, no food.

The Boxcars

The following day, December 21, each man was given a little piece of cheese and some crackers, and loaded onto small freight cars, or boxcars, sixty men to a car. At this point I was somehow separated from the other men in my squad. I never saw any of them again. The sliding door was locked with a piece of wire wound where a padlock would usually be placed. The sliding door on the other side had previously been nailed shut. My train pulled out at noon, heading farther into Germany. I found out later that some men in my company and battalion went to other destinations, on other trains.

I saw very few of the men in my company and don't know exactly what became of the rest. I do know that the great majority survived. After the war I received a postcard from First Lieutenant Jack Stein advising me that Staff Sergeant Bob King was among those killed during the battle, and that Tech Sergeant Jim Melton, Staff Sergeant Laverne Borrison, and Sergeant Grady Wise had died in captivity.

The sixty of us, probably all strangers to each other, crowded into the small, unheated boxcar. Some were walking wounded, and were allowed to stretch out in the middle of the floor. The rest of us sat around the sides, usually with our knees drawn up. We were all cold, hungry, miserable, and humiliated, and in a state of shock. Until several days ago, we had all been part of a powerful fighting force, and now we were reduced to dirty, hungry rabble. *How could we have done so badly?* we all wondered.

The train moved along, heading east, often stopping for

no apparent reason. We crossed the Rhine River on a long bridge at Koblenz. I began to hope we would get wherever we were going before our bombers or fighter planes took a bead on the train. I wondered if my parents and brothers and sisters knew about the battle, and that I had been in it. Or if they knew if I was dead or alive. As it turned out, I didn't learn the answer to that question for five months.

About 5:00 P.M. or so on December 23rd, it was already dark outside, and we had been parked for some time at the northern edge of a railroad marshaling yard outside the town of Limburg, Germany. We were all homesick and wishing we were all home for Christmas with our families.

Then one of the soldiers in the front of the boxcar began to sing "Silent Night." I couldn't see his face in the dark. He had a good voice and obviously had experience singing in a choir. It was a very moving experience.

"Silent night, holy night
All is calm, all is bright."

Just then a bright red light started to glow up ahead. We could see it through the small vent window near the top of the wall on the side of the boxcar. He stopped singing and we all started talking about what it could mean. We soon realized the light was from a flare dropped from a pathfinder plane. We were about to be bombed!

After many days of heavy overcast, the weather had cleared and British bombers were overhead! Their target was the railroad marshaling yard! Soon we heard and felt enormous explosions all around, and blinding light glowed through the vent windows. We all screamed and yelled to be let out of the boxcar. To our relief someone soon removed the wire locking the sliding door and we all tumbled out. At the time I assumed that the door had been unlocked by one of the

German guards, but I found out only recently that it had been unlocked by one of the prisoners. He was a very skinny fellow and squeezed out one of the vent windows in his car after breaking loose the barbed wire covering it. He or other prisoners then unlocked all the rest of the boxcars.

Straight ahead was a low hill, which turned out to be the side of a quarry, and some of the men from our boxcar started running up the side of it. Most of us chose to keep a low profile and began running back along the side of the train. All the while other men were pouring out of the other boxcars as bombs continued to explode with blinding light and earth-shaking concussion.

Following the crowd off to the right, I found myself running down an earthen ramp to the bottom of a quarry, where everyone was trying to squeeze into a tunnel along the side. I managed to get just inside the entrance next to one of the German guards and sweated out the rest of the bombing attack.

When the bombing finally ended, the guards ordered everyone to go back to the boxcars. When we got there, we found dead and wounded men lying around, but the train itself had sustained negligible damage. Our train stood at the north edge of the rail yard while most of the bombs hit and devastated the center of the rail yard. I found out later that one bomb hit a barracks building at a nearby P.O.W. camp, Stalag XII-A, and killed sixty American officers.

We were finally lined up and counted, and ordered to get back in the boxcars. But seven or eight men were missing from our group of sixty. And in the dark, I could dimly see some bodies lying on the hillside alongside our boxcar. We got back in, and gradually settled down, thanking our lucky stars we had survived.

After we were all quiet, someone said, "Hey, how about singing us some more songs?" There was only silence. . . . One of the men lying out on the hillside was the soldier who had just sung "Silent Night." It just broke my heart! What a waste! He didn't know it, but when he was singing to cheer us up, he had only minutes to live. He had sung his own requiem. Ever since, whenever I hear that song, I think of that poor young man. I experienced many horrors in battle and as a prisoner, but the waste of this young man's life that night almost brought me to tears.

The next day, Christmas Eve, the bodies were taken away in horse-drawn wagons. Later, a wagon loaded with loaves of bread arrived and the loaves were distributed among the prisoners. One loaf was shared by about six prisoners. We were also given some Red Cross food parcels to share. But there were so many of us that my share consisted of three or four prunes. They also let us out of the cars, one car at a time, under guard, to relieve ourselves. Until then steel helmets had to be used for that purpose.

We passed Christmas day locked in the boxcar. The train had not moved, no doubt because the track had to be repaired first. That was one of the worst possible ways I could think of to spend this day. I thought about home, my parents, my brothers and sisters, and my friends. I did some praying. And I worried that my mother and father, in particular, would not know what had happened to me.

Perhaps it was the next day when the train started moving again, and we were able to get some drinking water somewhere along the line when our train stopped at a station. Again, steel helmets were used to carry the water. Along the way I was able to determine that after we left Limburg, we passed through cities or towns, such as Fulda and Erfurt, always wondering what our final destination would be. And I'm sure we all wondered whether we would be bombed again, and whether we would survive.

Stalag IV-B at Muhlberg, Germany

On December 29, 1944, after eight days and nights in the dirty, smelly boxcars, our train arrived at a dismal, grim-looking, prisoner-of-war camp known by the Germans as Stalag IV-B. It was surrounded by a high barb-wire fence and wooden guard towers and searchlights. It turned out the camp was just east of the Elbe River, about three miles northeast of a little town called Muhlberg, about a hundred miles south of Berlin.

We were ordered out of the boxcars about noon on a bitterly cold, windy day. The guards herded us to an open area outside the camp and separated us into small groups so we could be guarded more easily. Soon the miserable cold started to chill us to the bone. How I regretted I had thrown away my overcoat during that killer forced march off the Schnee Eifel Ridge! We stood and stamped our feet and clapped our hands as the minutes, then the hours went by. The guards would be changed from time to time, but we just stood there all day long. We were chilled to the bone, hungry, thirsty, and forlorn.

Eight hours later, about 8:00 P.M., my group was taken to a barn inside the camp. Just before we entered, everyone was ordered to remove and put on separate piles all steel helmets and rubber overshoes. There was no heat inside, but at least there was no bitter wind whipping around our faces. I sat on a bale of hay and after a while, I took off my gloves and rubbed my hands to get circulation back. I also wanted to take off my combat boots so I could rub my feet. At first my fingers were too stiff from the cold to unbuckle and untie them, but eventually I made some progress. But as I started to remove one of the boots, I noticed my foot was swollen. I realized that if I took off my boot I wouldn't be able to get it back on again. So that was that.

Later, we were taken to a small building where we were taken in one at a time to be searched. I had a very hard time getting my boots off, and then back on. After I was searched, the methodical Germans gave me a receipt for some Belgian francs and my Social Security card.

Our group finally ended up in a combination cold shower and delousing building. No towels, we had to stand around in the cold room until we were dry enough to put our clothes back on. I shaved with a borrowed razor and then a British prisoner injected each of us in the chest with some drug. We earnestly hoped it wouldn't kill us.

After that a German soldier handed me a German dog tag embossed with my P.O.W. number, and I put it around my neck on the same chain with my U.S. Army dog tags. I was now a certified "Kriegsgefangener." Then, when it was my turn, I had a mug shot taken with my name and new German P.O.W. number, 312 199, chalked on a board in front of my chest, just as it's done at a police station back in the States.

(Some years later I was sent that mug shot. It turned out a British prisoner at Stalag IV-B had grabbed a bunch of these photos from the files as the German guards fled from the camp. I keep an enlargement of it around to remind me that whatever my present problems are, they pale in comparison to what I had to endure back then.)

By now, except for my feet, I had thawed out pretty well. Finally, we were brought into the main part of the camp and marched down the road to our new home, a barracks building filled with British prisoners of war. They were expecting our small group and gave us a warm welcome. They sat us down at a homemade table and gave each of us a slice of heavy German bread, some tea served in a tin can, and a cigarette. I think it was the first time I had relaxed in many days.

The Brits were an impressive bunch. All those in my barracks were corporals or sergeants in the Royal Air Force and had all bailed out of crippled aircraft. They had been prisoners for one or two or more years, and yet had "stiff upper lips" and maintained good military discipline. By comparison our group was a somewhat motley crowd, disheveled and still in shock, and virtually all strangers to one another.

All the bunks were full, but our British hosts doubled up a bit so we Americans could sleep, two to a single bunk, in a group by ourselves. The mattress was a large cloth bag filled with straw. I fell into a deep sleep.

The next thing I knew, it was early morning and a British airman was coming along, hitting each double bunk with a club, shouting, "On parade!" It was Reveille, Royal Air Force style. We all quickly filed out to a big, open area along with thousands of other British and American soldiers. We didn't have to get dressed first, because at least we Americans slept in the only clothes we had. Here we were lined up to be counted by the German guards. It was a long process, and the Germans were very meticulous in making sure the entire count was absolutely correct.

Each day was like the one before. Reveille and a long head count. Back in the barracks, you could eventually expect a tin can full of lukewarm, ersatz coffee—if you could beg or borrow a spare tin can. In a day or so, I became the proud owner of one myself, with a homemade tin handle.

Then, between 10:00 A.M. and 11:00 A.M., some British soldiers would show up carrying large buckets of what they called "skilly," a watery soup made with turnips. Each of us would get a one-tin-can serving.

Late in the afternoon each day, everyone would get about a seventh of a loaf of hard, sour bread, several very small cooked potatoes, a teaspoon of sugar or jam, a tin cup of tea, and maybe a pat of some strange tasting margarine. And on alternate days, either a tablespoon-size piece of what was probably horsemeat or a similar size piece of cheese. That was it for the day, every day.

The barracks were one-story, long wooden buildings, divided into two sections separated by a room with wash basins and cold-water taps. It was hard to keep clean. I did acquire a razor, but I don't recall having a towel at this time. And I know I didn't have a toothbrush for five months. But I really lucked out when the British gave me a well-worn Polish Army overcoat. I often wondered what had happened to the previous owner.

The latrine was a large unheated concrete outhouse not far from my barracks, available only during daylight hours. At night all that was available was an in-house outhouse near the door including a five-gallon bucket. The very first time I had the "skilly" soup, I was hit with the "G.I.s." For the next several days, between visits to the concrete outhouse and the in-house bucket, I scoured trash heaps in bitter cold, looking for the smallest scrap of paper. I never found one and was one filthy, miserable lost soul.

During daylight hours we were free to roam the British compound. There were other compounds holding prisoners of many nationalities, including Russians, Italians, Frenchmen, Belgians, and Dutchmen. The camp was overloaded, and included about 8,000 British, 4,000 American, and 10,000 prisoners of other nationalities. The British prisoners came from not just England but from Scotland, Wales, Northern Ireland, Australia, Canada, New Zealand, and elsewhere.

We soon found out that in a prison camp, cigarettes were used as money, as a means of exchange. This worked because they were both scarce and desired. Once, I bought a small pocket knife from a fellow G.I. for three cigarettes. Later, I got a fork and a spoon the same way from a prisoner from some other country. And a few poor souls who just had to have a nicotine fix would sell their tin cup of soup or their bread allotment for one or two cigarettes.

One day I was going from one barracks to another, looking for friends. I happened upon a group of G.I.s who had been identified as Jewish. They had been segregated from all the rest. I found out long after the war that some of these men might have suffered and died under horrible circumstances. If the Germans had later transferred some or all of them to Stalag IX-B, they then would have ended up at Berga am Elster, a notorious death camp. With only starvation rations, these American soldiers were worked to death digging a tunnel into the side of a hill with primitive tools under the supervision of merciless, brutal guards.

George Zak, new young soldier.

Limburg railyard, Germany, after the bombing (courtesy of USAF Museum).

Main entrance to Stalag IV-B (courtesy of Collectie Rijksmuseum, Amsterdam).

A group of newly arrived POWs (courtesy of Collectie Rijksmuseum, Amsterdam).

Some Americans captured in the Battle of the Bulge (courtesy of Collectie Rijksmuseum, Amsterdam).

George Zak, prisoner of war.

Watchtower No. 2 (courtesy of Collectie Rijksmuseum, Amsterdam).

Propaganda photo of Russian POWs (courtesy of Collectie Rijksmuseum, Amsterdam).

Dresden, Germany, after the firebombing (courtesy of Imperial War Museum, London).

German soldiers collecting bodies (courtesy of Imperial War Museum, London).

Bodies awaiting cremation (courtesy of Imperial War Museum, London).

One of many funeral pyres (courtesy of Imperial War Museum, London).

Ceremony at Stalag IV-B honoring the late President Roosevelt (courtesy of Achim Kilian).

American and other flags flying at Stalag IV-B after liberation by the Russians (courtesy of Achim Kilian).

George and Bob Zak, two brothers together again.

Joan and George Zak—a toast to life and love!

Our young family.

Our family today.

Dresden and the Blanket Factory at Lobau

We new arrivals who were privates or privates first class were being sent out in groups for work somewhere or another, on what the Germans called *"arbeit kommandos."* So on January 9, 1945, I found myself on a passenger train as one of a group of thirty-five men, including some former A.S.T.P. types like myself, heading south, destined for who knows where. We had one car of the train to ourselves along with several guards.

Several hours later we found our train traveling through the outskirts of a very large, impressive old city, and finally came to a stop on an elevated track outside a huge train station. We were dumfounded. We had heard all about the fantastic bombing of German cities by our Eighth Air Force, and here was a giant metropolis without a visible scratch! Could we all have been duped by false Allied propaganda, we wondered? By now we knew the name of this city was Dresden, and we were at Dresden Central Station.

One of the smarter members of the group recalled that he had read somewhere that Dresden had been spared bombing because it was a hospital center and had no significant military industry. That seemed a reasonable explanation to the rest of us, and we regained our faith in the Eighth Air Force.

Our train sat there for a long time, apparently waiting for its turn to enter the station. I stared out the window, taking in everything around me. Just below, a group of women were waiting for a streetcar, and just about every one of them was wearing a black armband. The war had not come to Dresden, but the men of Dresden had gone to the war.

Our train finally entered the station, and we were herded to a small waiting room until it was time to board our next train. As we passed through the busy main concourse, I was astounded to see how life seemed so normal here. There were soldiers on leave as well as civilians coming or going, but I also saw one young man in civilian clothes pass us carrying a pair of skis over his shoulder.

While sitting in the waiting room, I found on the bench a pamphlet written in English, which had an article lauding a heroic German woman test pilot. She supposedly survived a ride in an unarmed V-1 rocket to find out why the guidance system wasn't working properly. This sounded like pure propaganda to me. It has been said that in war the first casualty is the truth.

We finally boarded our train and started heading east, and after a relatively short ride, we arrived at our new home, the quaint little town of Lobau. We knew we were now in eastern Germany, about thirty-five miles east of Dresden and about fifteen miles from the border of German-occupied Czechoslovakia.

Our group of thirty-five, all strangers to each other, were marched to what looked like a barn. It had been converted into a *lager,* or prison, and had a steel entrance door. The interior looked clean and new, and had double wooden bunks and an old stove for heat. A washroom with a cold-water tap and a privy was at the far end. Not bad. After we entered the *lager,* a German *hauptmann,* or captain, announced in heavily-accented English that we were going to be put to work at the local blanket factory. He laid down some rules and told us we would be shot if we fraternized with any German women. Feldwebel (Sergeant) Mueller and his guards would be in charge of us. Two of the prisoners spoke German, and one was made our official interpreter.

The next day we were marched to the factory and put to

work, six days a week. Most of us worked most of the time weaving army blankets on mechanical looms. You had to load small packets of spun wool into a foot-long narrow wooden box, pointed on both ends, called a shuttlecock. The wool would trail out a hole in the box. Wooden paddles on the left and right would then propel the box back and forth, interweaving the spun wool with strong threads to form blanket material. The finished blanket material ended up on a six-foot-wide roll under the table.

The German lady in charge explained in sign language that whenever one of these threads broke, it had to be retied with a special knot. She tried to teach us how to tie it, but we all agreed, just to bug her, to pretend not to understand. That meant that when a thread broke she had to be summoned to repair it. She got quite angry that we Americans were so stupid.

So we settled into this routine and I think most of us realized we were lucky we hadn't been sent like many others on a work party doing hard labor under primitive conditions. We also realized this could all change at any time.

We were also pleased that since we were working, we received, in addition to small amounts of bread, potatoes, and meat or cheese, two bowls of soup each day instead of only one, and it was decent soup made of potatoes or barley.

And during the months we were there, we shared a number of eleven-pound food parcels prepared in the United States, England, or Canada, and delivered to us by way of the International Red Cross. Those parcels were lifesavers. The parcels varied somewhat, but contained items such as powdered milk, corned beef, cheese, chocolate bars, cigarettes, butter, and tea leaves. When these parcels arrived from time to time, each parcel was shared by two men.

But we were still hungry all the time and spent a lot of time daydreaming about food. We were all losing weight and our pants were now too big around the waist. Once I received a Hershey bar from one of those food parcels, and ate just one square a day until it was all gone. I saved the small white paper wrapper and then every night for days thereafter I would have a sniff of the scent of chocolate.

By now, the middle of January 1945, both the German soldiers and the civilians knew the war was going badly for them. Although the German army had great initial success in their devastating attack through the Ardennes, later known as the Battle of the Bulge, it was being pushed back with great loss of men and equipment. And the Russian army was in Poland, coming ever closer to Germany from the east.

I believed this had a great effect on them. They realized that either the Russians or the Americans would soon be on their doorsteps. Feldwebel Mueller and his guards treated us decently and over time some even tried to win our favor.

My feet were still bothering me, and I complained to Mueller that I needed medical attention. To my surprise he arranged for a guard to take me to a local medical clinic. When we arrived I encountered a very beautiful blond girl about my age who fixed me with eyes burning with hatred. I could understand why she felt such rage at an enemy soldier. Possibly her father or brothers had met a bad end in battle somewhere. So much for fraternizing with the enemy.

A doctor examined both my feet and then lightly bandaged each one with a paper bandage. I put my boots on with some difficulty and then trudged back to the lager with my guard. So that was that. When I got back inside, I unwrapped and threw away the paper bandages. My feet would have to recover on their own.

Life as a prisoner of war was a pretty miserable, uncertain existence. We were hungry most of the time, and we were treated as nameless, laboring robots. And the Russians were coming! Would we be killed in the middle of the battle between the Germans and the Russians? Or would the German High Command order the execution of all prisoners? Or would the conquering Russians kill us or send us to a Russian prison camp? None of us knew, but we often thought the worst. But we sometimes realized, at least I know I did, that as bad as this was, we could have died a horrible, lingering death in battle. And somewhere out there, far to the west, this was happening every day to many other young American men still carrying on the fight.

One of the worst concerns I had was that my parents and brothers and sisters might not know what had become of me. Did they know I was alive? If so, did they worry that I might be suffering from grievous wounds? I knew my mother would be taking it all very badly. And I had no way to find out what was going on back home. From time to time, I would be overcome by homesickness and I despaired that I would never see my family and friends again.

In spite of the pressure we were all under, I think the thirty-five of us got along remarkably well. We were cooped up together every evening, and all day on Sunday, and sometimes there were minor flare-ups or cross words. But we were always in solidarity against the enemy.

One of the men was a real nicotine addict and was always dying for a smoke. Whenever we were walking to or from the factory, he would look for cigarette butts along the road. Once in a while, he would find one. Finally, he took up smoking tea leaves from a Red Cross package, and his teeth gradually developed a dark green stain.

The Germans did allow us to write a brief letter every few weeks, and in order to put my parents more at ease, I implied in my letters that the life of a prisoner was not bad at all, almost like vacationing at a resort. Still, I had no great faith that these letters were actually going anywhere.

(I found out after the war that the first of these letters

71

arrived at my parents' home in mid-April 1945, four months after my capture. I also found out that my parents had received a telegram from the War Department about ten days after my capture advising that I was "Missing in Action." Some weeks later, because there was no evidence of my death, they were sent a telegram advising that I was probably a prisoner of war. It was not until May that they received confirmation from the War Department that I had indeed been a prisoner of war since December.)

(And it turned out I had unwittingly caused my parents additional grief by sending home letters from the front line in Germany written as if I were still in England. I did this so they wouldn't be so worried about me. So when they got the "Missing in Action" telegram, they were sure it was a mistake. My father spent a lot of time phoning and visiting army headquarters in Chicago before the family finally believed I really was missing in action.)

And there was no such thing as incoming mail.

(I also found out after the war that all letters sent to me via the International Red Cross, as specified by the War Department, were returned undelivered, stamped "Return to Sender, By Direction of the War Department, Undeliverable as Addressed.")

So the days wore on. We knew in a general way that the German army was being pushed back into Germany in the west by the American and British armies, and that the Russian army was relentlessly approaching from the east. It was still the middle of a bitter winter, and I felt sorry that our soldiers had to fight under such miserable conditions.

It was early in February, as I recall, that we started to hear thunderous artillery fire off to the east. The Russians were coming closer and closer. One day our windows were shaking from the concussion. Suddenly the road near our lager was filled with a long caravan of heavy artillery pieces being pulled by trucks or horses, headed for the front. After a day or so, the noise of artillery faded away. Apparently the Russians had been forced back.

Late in the evening on February 13, 1945, some of our guards came into the lager and rousted us out. We were led across to the basement of the nearby bakery and told to stay there. An air raid was expected. No bombs fell on Lobau, but after some time, we could see from the window a great fire lighting the sky off to the west. We knew some place somewhere was taking a terrible pounding. After several hours we were led back to the lager and went to sleep wondering what had happened.

The next morning one of the guards came in and said, "Dresden kaput!" I remember the mixed feeling I had at the time. I hated the Nazis and all who helped them, but I felt heartsick thinking of the thousands of more-or-less innocent people who must have been blown to bits or incinerated. And I thought about those women I saw in Dresden a month earlier with the black armbands, waiting for a streetcar. Black armbands and all, their bodies were probably lying in or under the rubble. Knowing that Dresden was about thirty-five miles away, I was in awe that we could see the fire from this distance. It must have been a fantastic fire, roaring for miles in every direction! It was beyond my imagination.

A few days later, our entire group of thirty-five was taken to a large home or building of some kind and put to work bringing down from the attic a huge supply of paper bandages that had been stored there. We loaded these packets of bandages on an open-bed truck. I was astounded that the truck was powered by a wood-burning stove mounted on the truck bed just behind the driver's cab. The stove was connected by small pipes to the truck's engine. I had no idea how the energy from the stove powered the engine, but it did tell me that the Third Reich was running out of gasoline. We later found out that the bandages were destined for injured survivors of the devastating firestorm at Dresden.

We prisoners were of course coming and going in and out of the building as we loaded the truck and one of the guards suddenly panicked. He wasn't sure of the head count and thought some of us had escaped. He knew that if that had happened, he would be in serious trouble. The frightened guard confronted me and several others, screaming and shouting. His finger was on the trigger of the pistol that he pointed at us, and he looked as if he thought we were going to rush him. I froze, not moving a muscle, knowing that if any of us made the slightest move, he would start shooting wildly. He finally calmed down and realized all were accounted for. We all gave a sigh of relief and went back to loading the truck. A prisoner's life was, at best, a fragile and uncertain one.

Some days later, instead of working in the factory, we were divided into several groups and put to work with picks and shovels. Some were put to work at a garbage dump and gravel pit. In my case I was in a group taken to the front of a small hospital. Here we were put to work for several weeks digging a long, saw-toothed, six-foot deep trench to be used as an air raid shelter. The cold wasn't so severe at this time, but the hard digging was tough on young men who had all lost weight on the small rations we had to get by on. By this time I was down to around 120 to 125 pounds. One day I was thrilled to find a large, partially rotten turnip in a pile of refuse by the hospital. I ate the good part on the spot.

One day we were taking a break alongside our trench, and along the road came a most strange sight. Several horse-drawn wagons were passing slowly by, filled with a most unlikely group of "German" soldiers. These "German" soldiers, in Wehrmacht uniforms, carrying German rifles, were in fact Russians! More exactly, they were Soviets, but from some non-Russian part of the Soviet Union. They all had heavy, black mustaches and a swarthy complexion, and had no expression whatsoever on their faces.

The war had made some strange bedfellows. These men, possibly taken prisoner by the Germans earlier in the war, had volunteered to fight against the Communists. They were all doomed. They had no future. They didn't have long to live. I knew, and surely they knew, that if the victorious Russian army got its hands on them, they would be shot on the spot.

As the German army was being pushed back by the Russian army, now in Poland, the little town of Lobau was being prepared for battle with the Russian army. German army engineers began erecting a ten-foot-high log fence between the buildings on the outskirts of town. And the boys of the Hitler Youth Organization, smartly dressed in their uniforms, and carrying picks and shovels, marched by one day singing a patriotic song.

When our work party returned to our lager late the next day, we found that a gun pit with a ramp had been dug next to the wall of our lager. It was all ready for an artillery piece to be wheeled in, to be pointed at the road.

Another day, as our group was being marched by, we saw a huge artillery shell on a large wheelbarrow, about to be lowered into a deep pit dug at the base of a bridge spanning some railroad tracks. The bridge would be destroyed when the Russians approached.

All the preparations struck me as so futile, so insane. When the Russian army steamrolled in, it would make quick work of these feeble defenses and the still determined but crumbling German army. And the local German civilians would soon reap the whirlwind because of their country's fanatical support of Hitler and all the atrocities inflicted in his name on the Russian population. I wondered how badly that beautiful young blond girl I ran into at the medical clinic would be treated when some drunken, vengeful Russian soldiers found her.

The Quarry near Hohnstein

March finally came and the worst of winter was over. And what a bitter-cold winter it had been! I learned later that it had been one of the most severe winters in many years.

One day—I believe it was March 10, 1945—we were told to get our few belongings together. We were leaving. Destination unknown.

I don't recall if we took a train part of the way or not, but we walked much of the way, guarded by German soldiers. One night we were locked up with some British prisoners in a large building. Two days later, on March 12, we finally entered a small prison camp in a forest near the Elbe River, somewhere near the town of Hohnstein, a few miles southeast of Dresden.

The sign by the entrance gate indicated the camp was a part of the Stalag IV-A system. As we entered we saw it was a bleak place surrounded by barbed wire. As we lined up inside to be counted, we saw an American prisoner passing nearby. He was walking with his shoulders slumped; his face was dirty. One of us shouted to him, asking, "What kind of a place is this?" He didn't answer. Uh-oh.

I noticed that all the prisoners in the camp were American soldiers. Our group was assigned to several small wooden barracks, with a bunk available for each man. The "latrine" was a ditch near one of the barb-wire fences. The only water available outside the off-limits kitchen building came from a pipe extending along the ground some distance away. Not far away from the barracks was a small rock quarry. This didn't look good.

We were then taken, a few at a time, inside a wooden building where, to my surprise, we were each given a short physical exam by a Polish doctor, himself a prisoner. My buddy Larkin Mayfield was found to have some kind of heart problem, and I had jaundice. In a combination of Polish, German, and English, the doctor told me he could flunk me if I wanted, and gave me a choice: stay here and work or be sent to Stalag IV-B. He warned me that he had heard that conditions had gotten worse at IV-B.

I knew if I stayed in this camp I would have to do hard labor and would probably get even further rundown. On the other hand, if I traveled back to Stalag IV-B, I might be killed on the train by strafing Russian or American fighter planes. And maybe things would be worse if and when I got there. But I decided my best bet was to go back.

So Mayfield and I were excused from work and sat around for two weeks waiting to be transferred back to Stalag IV-B at Muhlberg just east of the Elbe River. The rest of the men spent each day doing pick-and-shovel work, mostly repairing railroad tracks somewhere outside the camp.

One of my memories of those two weeks was my loathing of an American G.I. who had been put in charge of all the prisoners by the Germans. He looked very-well fed and was enjoying himself ordering the rest of us around.

One day I wandered into a small, roofless, concrete block building. Possibly meant to be a latrine some day. To my shock and horror, a stretcher was on the floor with a blanket-covered body. It was obviously the body of a prisoner who had just died. But the form under the blanket was so thin the poor guy must have died of dysentery or something else that had wasted his body.

I wanted to uncover his face, but I just could not. His face, too, would have been emaciated. I sat on the floor for about a half an hour thinking about this young man. His worst fears had been realized. He wouldn't be going home, and no loved one was by his side during his final days and hours. I finally left, offering a silent prayer for him and his family.

Another vivid memory I have was of a night the air raid siren was wailing. All camp lights were turned off and we were under strict orders not to leave our barracks. It happened I had an urgent need to use our open-air latrine and I decided to sneak over to it in the dark. I got about twenty feet out the door when a rifle bullet snapped right by my ear, courtesy of a German guard just outside the barb-wire fence. I swung around and made it back to the barracks in about two seconds, expecting a second bullet in my back as I ran. I guess I was inside before he could get off a second shot.

One day we received some Red Cross food parcels, and we each got a can of meat or powdered milk and other items, and felt very rich. One of the guys from our Lobau group approached me and proposed we make an escape. He said he could last at least a week on a can of meat and a little bread. But where would we go? And neither of us spoke any language besides English. And I didn't like the idea of being hunted down by the SS soldier in the black uniform who patrolled the outer perimeter of the camp with two vicious dogs. I said no. And he didn't go either. A wise decision.

Dresden Again and Back to Stalag IV-B at Muhlberg

So on March 27, 1945, Larkin Mayfield and I, and several other American soldiers, escorted by guards, made our way on foot for some distance and finally boarded a train. In a relatively short time, I realized our train was heading into the ruins of Dresden! Just forty days ago, this was the scene of a modern-day Dante's Inferno! God only knew how many soldiers and civilians had been killed by bombs or were burned to death or suffocated in the great firestorm.

When I was here previously, on January 9, just eleven weeks ago, I had looked out in awe at a huge, beautiful, rather majestic old city. But now! Our train came into what had been the center of the city on a newly-repaired elevated track, and stopped outside the ruins of the Central Station. A new wooden stair led up to the track.

Everywhere I looked there was utter devastation. Block after block, mile after mile, there was nothing but rubble. Huge stones and bricks from major buildings were piled in great heaps. Only parts of fire-scorched outer walls stood among the debris. I could make out where the streets had been only because the piles of bricks and stones were not as high there.

And what of the people? The only living ones I could see were a small cluster of workers trying to clear a path by hand down a street next to the ruins of the railroad terminal. What a hopeless task. And where were the rest? Where were those women I saw when I was here before, the ones with the black armbands? As I had earlier imagined, they were somewhere in or under the rubble, along with their children. This once thriving city was now a giant, ghastly, silent graveyard.

My mind was filled with many conflicting thoughts. Of man's inhumanity to man. Of the absolute evil of war. Of that depraved monster, Adolph Hitler, who brought it all on. Of the tens of millions of Germans who shared his view of a Master Race with a God-given right to slaughter all who got in the way. And yet in my own heart and soul, I felt some shame and guilt.

(I was astounded to learn after the war that about 135,000 people died that night at Dresden, far more than the 80,000 who died when the atomic bomb was dropped at Hiroshima six months later.)

Our train finally moved on, away from this horrible Armageddon, and later that day our guards led us back into the dismal confines of Stalag IV-B. I was "home" again.

Larkin Mayfield and I were assigned to the same barracks I had been in back in late December and early January. The big difference this time was that there were no bunks available. So we got permission from the British barracks leader to use a small, narrow, homemade table for a place to sleep at night. By now we were both very skinny, but the table was barely wide enough for us to sleep on our sides facing the same way. We used our overcoats, one for a mattress and the other for a blanket. It still beat sleeping outside.

As for night clothing, it was the same as day clothing. We both wore the same outfit day and night, around the clock. Four months after being captured, we were still wearing the clothes we were captured in. We had razors for some time now, but neither of us had a toothbrush. But now I could at least take a cold "bird bath" every day, and wash my clothes once in a while, after a fashion. The Brits had adequate clothing, but some of us Americans looked more like skid row derelicts than soldiers.

Soon after I arrived at Stalag IV-B, I noticed a very itchy

rash had developed around the front of my waist. I went to the infirmary and was told I had scabies, parasitic mites that burrow under the skin. I also found out these mites usually only attack cattle. Great. So this is what I had been reduced to. They gave me some salve for it and eventually it all cleared up.

After we settled in, I could see that the Polish doctor was wrong about Stalag IV-B. Conditions had not gotten worse; they were about the same as before. Things were not good, but they weren't horrible. And I didn't have to work. The skimpy food was still the biggest problem. And I was now back to just one tin can of turnip soup a day instead of the two when I worked at the blanket factory at Lobau.

(Recently I had the pleasure of meeting and talking with Ted Basel, one of the men I had left behind at the pick and shovel camp. From what he told me about the rather miserable time they had after I had left, I believe I had made the right choice in having the Polish doctor flunk me on my physical.)

The weather had turned mild and I was now able to enjoy the fresh air. I struck up a friendship with an English sergeant in the Royal Air Force and we would take daily walks around the compound. He was an intelligent, soft-spoken fellow who had been a prisoner for several years. It was fascinating for me to draw out stories from him about what it had been like fighting the Germans at a time when the war was going so badly. I also discovered he had a hand-washing obsession. He washed his hands many times every day. Maybe he was afraid of catching something from me.

One day all the Americans in the British compound were assembled in an open area and told by the British leaders that volunteers were needed to be sent to Leipzig on an *arbeit kommando*. It would be a pick-and-shovel job, cleaning up damage from air raids. The good part of the deal was that Leipzig was a lot closer to the advancing American army. The idea of being in a large city at this time didn't appeal to me at all, and the first chance I got, I slipped around a barracks building and out of sight.

On April 13, 1945, word spread through the camp that President Franklin Roosevelt had died the day before. It was sad, stunning news. He had been our inspirational leader and did not live to savor the almost-certain-to-come victory over our enemies. The British compound, in which many Americans like myself also resided, immediately organized and put on a very impressive, moving memorial service. Everyone in the compound was turned out for the service, and the Brits with the best uniforms marched in majestic, stirring fashion. We Americans, in our shabby uniforms, and without any designated leaders, were put to shame.

There was at least one radio hidden somewhere in the British compound, and the highlight of every evening was the report about the progress of the war read aloud in every barracks. The German army was being crushed by American forces pressing from the west and by Russian forces coming from the east. It couldn't last long now, but so far there was no sign of the war in our area.

Possibly it was the day after the memorial service was held for President Roosevelt, when I volunteered for a work party to push a large empty wagon under guard to the railroad station at Muhlberg to bring back a load of Red Cross food parcels. These parcels did not arrive often enough and this was great news.

It was about three miles to town, and along the way there and back, we could see a group of German soldiers training in a field. There were large wooden targets painted to resemble enemy tanks, and the soldiers were being taught how to attack them with their version of an anti-tank bazooka rocket that they called a *panzerfaust.*

Shortly after we passed the training field on the way back, we were startled to hear machine-gun fire. We all turned and saw a fighter plane strafing the field where the German soldiers had been training. We couldn't see the soldiers at this point, but we could all imagine the terror and chaos that struck those hapless men. I never found out for sure whether the plane was American or Russian. The air war had arrived near the Elbe River and Stalag IV-B, and we prisoners of war were going to have front-row seats!

From that point on, the entire mood at the camp changed. Up to now, liberation from captivity had only been a distant dream. Not anymore. Now it was a real possibility!

Early each morning a German fighter plane would fly over our camp, only about two hundred feet over our heads, heading south. Soon two Allied fighter planes would arrive in our area and start machine-gunning any targets of opportunity they could find. Shortly after they left, that same German fighter plane would zoom over our camp heading back north again. I couldn't decide what the German pilot was up to. He seemed to be getting out of the area to keep from being shot down, or possibly he didn't want the plane destroyed on the ground.

One day I heard a very loud explosion coming from beyond the other end of camp. I made my way down there and British soldiers pointed out a freight train on fire about a half a mile away across the open field. They explained that the train had been strafed and had caught fire. Later, the last car had exploded. I had nothing better to do, so I stood around and watched. Suddenly there was another tremendous explosion and the next freight car was gone! The train must have been loaded with ammunition or other explosives. There were no German planes around and the Allied planes were having a field day.

Another day I was walking around the open area and I noticed two planes were dive-bombing some kind of facility to the north of our camp. It was quite a distance away and I could not tell exactly what the target was. As the first plane went into a steep dive toward the target, I could see small black puffs of smoke and small bright lights sparkling near it. This was anti-aircraft fire coming from the ground. The plane completed its dive and pulled up and away.

The second plane was following right behind, on exactly the same path. As it pulled up again, I could see some black smoke trailing behind. It had been hit! It flew off to the east still trailing smoke and disappeared. I wondered why the second pilot had given the gunners on the ground such an easy target by coming in on the very same path as the first plane. I hoped he made it back to his air base.

The day was bright and clear. I was standing outdoors with a group of American and British men when we began to hear the drone of planes. Looking up we soon saw a large formation of American bombers heading right in the direction of our camp. The planes were flying low enough for us to make out the silhouettes of the nearest ones. It was a very impressive and a very deadly-looking sight. Somewhere, someplace, the Germans were going to take a terrible beating!

Suddenly a large flare came spilling out of the lead plane, heading right for us. We were the target! Our camp and everybody in it was going to be obliterated! God help us all! As we stared in shocked horror, we saw the lead plane and the ones following begin making a turn to their right. So the flare was just a turning marker! We all started breathing again and thanked God the bombs were going to be dropped somewhere else.

One morning I was standing around with other men in our barracks, wondering what the day would bring, when suddenly we heard the sound of machine-gun bullets hitting our roof! At first I had thought it was hail. We all hit the floor. Machine gun bullets! Had the Germans opened fire from the guard towers? The firing only lasted a few seconds. No one was hurt and we all went outside to see what had happened.

Men were milling around, and we soon found out that an Allied fighter plane had strafed a prisoner work party on the road that was bringing firewood back to the camp. Some of the bullets hit the camp as well. I don't recall exactly what casualties were suffered on the road, but an American in the barracks across from ours was killed instantly by a .50-caliber bullet through his chest.

The Russians Arrive at Stalag IV-B

On the afternoon of April 22, 1945, I was walking near the fence outside the buildings housing the German guards. What looked like the entire German guard unit was standing in several rows being inspected by their officers. They had their rifles, steel helmets, and packs on their backs. They looked very ready. But for what?

The next morning, April 23, we got up and went out to the open area for the usual morning count by the German guards. But no Germans! They had all left the camp! We were on our own!

One of the gates to the camp was not far away, and a number of us gravitated to it. It was open! Some men were standing outside and I joined them. It was a thrilling moment! I was now outside the prison camp. I was no longer a prisoner! I was overcome by great joy and exaltation, and I felt a great burden lift from my shoulders. I was no longer German P.O.W. Number 312 199, but a free man!

I realized how lucky I had been not to have been killed or wounded, or to have contracted dysentery or some other disease. And I thought of the many brave men who had. And then I began to wonder what would happen next.

I didn't have long to wait. For, off to the northeast I could see a long horse-drawn wagon caravan heading west. The Russians were coming! As those of us outside the gate stared at this strange sight, we noticed four men on horseback had left the caravan and were heading straight for us.

In just a few minutes, the four horsemen rode up to the

gate and slowed their horses to a walk. We all gaped with our mouths open as these strange men passed by. They looked like Cossack cavalrymen to me. They wore quilted coats, cloth caps, had fierce-looking mustaches, and carried submachine guns on a sling over their shoulders. They had the stoic air of veterans of many battles, had no expression on their faces, and completely ignored us. The four horsemen disappeared into the camp, leaving all of us somewhat stunned and amazed. I never saw those horsemen again.

I eventually wandered back into the camp and was standing near the gate when I saw a stream of Russian prisoners of war running out of the gate and heading east at a fast pace. The ones who passed near me had a look of fear and panic on their faces. One Russian prisoner, who didn't realize the gate was open, was trying to tear open a hole in the barb-wire fence with his bare hands.

It was clear to me that these men had been ordered by the four Russian horsemen to leave the camp at once and start heading east. In the Russian view, any soldier who allowed himself to be captured was a traitor to the cause and had to be dealt with very harshly. I was sure their future was very bleak.

I went back to my barracks and found a new electricity in the air as the British and American prisoners talked excitedly about their new freedom and the coming of the Russians. Soon Russian soldiers could be seen coming and going about the camp, and we were now under new but somewhat untrustworthy management.

Some of the men in the camp went on foraging missions outside the camp and brought back live chickens and whatever other food they could find and had little private feasts. The rest of us continued to get along on the same skimpy food we were used to. One group reported they found that an old couple at a nearby farm had hung themselves. I guessed they could not imagine living under the heel of the conquering Russians.

As I wandered around the camp, I happened to come upon Russian soldiers escorting a small group of newly-captured German soldiers into the camp. I watched as the Russians took them to the small concrete jail that the Germans had used to lock up troublesome prisoners of war. The German soldiers looked grim and exhausted, just as we Americans must have looked when we were captured. I felt some grim satisfaction as I stared at them, but somehow I still felt sorry for them.

We soon found that the common Russian soldiers in the camp were generally friendly, but I was wary of the intentions of the Russian officers now in charge of us. The Russians were technically our allies, but were known to be difficult partners with an agenda of their own. It was well known that the partnership with the Western Powers was strictly a marriage of convenience. I wanted to get away from their control and back to the American lines as soon as possible.

With the Russians and American Army Reps at Riesa

On the evening of April 25, 1945, two days after the Russians had arrived, several American jeeps pulled up outside the gate. It turned out they were part of a patrol that had crossed the Elbe River about ten miles south of our camp at the town of Strehla and were on their way north to contact the Russian army at Torgau. But it was great to see some fellow American soldiers who weren't prisoners. They looked very healthy and well fed, and seemed relaxed and confident. A bunch of us gathered around and tried to find out what they knew about our situation. They didn't have a clue.

All of a sudden, I noticed that the rear bumpers on the jeeps bore the stenciled marking "69 XX." These men were from the Sixty-ninth Infantry Division, my brother Bob's outfit! Could Bob be in the area? Had he been killed or wounded? Was he okay? The last I had heard, he and the Sixty-ninth Infantry Division were still back in the States! I found a scrap of paper, borrowed a pencil, and wrote my name and my brother's name and unit on it. I told one of the soldiers about my brother, gave him my note, and asked him to get word to Bob that I was okay and where I was. The soldier didn't seem too interested, but stuck the note in a pocket. I found out later on that he apparently never did anything about it.

Ten days later, on May 5, the Russians announced to the British camp leaders that the Americans and British would be immediately escorted to a new location south of the camp. We were given a pack of American cigarettes and some candy and

89

started out on foot about noon. We walked at a leisurely pace and took rest stops along the way. Where the cigarettes and candy came from, I never knew. And I never heard what became of the other prisoners left behind.

We came upon a wrecked bridge at the town of Strehla on the Elbe River about 6:00 P.M. The Russians had removed a large minefield the Germans had planted and had cleared an open path to the bridge. Although the bridge had been damaged, it was still usable. This was the same bridge the American patrol had used to cross over the Elbe River in the other direction a week earlier.

About 8:30 P.M. we arrived at the city of Riesa on the western side of the Elbe River and were escorted by the Russians to an abandoned former German army compound on the outskirts of town. The compound had been an engineering school and it included four large, multistory brick barracks buildings and an adjoining mess hall. We all soon had our own beds. What an improvement over the wooden table Larkin Mayfield and I had shared as a bed for the past month!

During that night I was often awakened by the sound of Russian tanks and artillery rumbling through town. This continued all the next day. There was still a war to fight. And the next day the Russians had us all register with them, giving basic information about ourselves. I wasn't exactly sure what they were going to do with this information, but I hoped it was to be forwarded to the Allied armies.

The Russians started to provide food for us. Once they brought a pig and slaughtered it on the edge of the street, and it wasn't long before all the meat ended up in some soup. But otherwise all I could get to eat was peas, potatoes and rice, then more peas, potatoes and rice. Once a bunch of us found a barrel of pickles, but as hard as I tried, I could not eat one. I was hungry as could be, but I could not seem to digest anything at all. My stomach was a mess. How I longed for a bowl of milk and corn flakes.

Mayfield and I and several other G.I.s wandered into Riesa to see if we could find something to eat that we could digest. We came upon a friendly Russian soldier riding a bike with his submachine gun slung over his shoulder. We asked him in sign language where we could find some food.

He understood, took us to a nearby house, and led us in, where we encountered several terrified German women. One of them was carrying an infant in her arms. Ignoring them he took us down the basement stairs and pointed to a large cardboard carton. How he knew about it I don't know. He must have been there before. We opened it and found it full of cans of evaporated milk! We were jubilant! We hadn't had any milk in at least five months, except for a small amount of powdered KLIM milk from Red Cross parcels.

Just as we started to take cans out of the box, the German woman rushed down the stairs still carrying her baby and cried out in German that the milk was for her baby. We had a dilemma. We were all skinny, half-starved, and malnourished, but the baby needed milk too. I told the guys to take only one can each, and leave the rest for the baby. They agreed, and we left. We each cut open our can and walked along the street drinking the heavenly fluid.

Later we tried another house, which proved to be abandoned and empty. But I did find and carry away with me a small blank notebook and pencil. Beginning that night I started writing brief notes about past events and dates, and I started keeping a daily log. I still have that notebook, and it has been very helpful to me while writing this chronicle.

On May 7, 1945, the Russians had us all register again. We wondered what was going on. Later, we Americans were all lined up and it was announced that a Russian woman doctor was going to check us all for venereal diseases. This caused quite an uproar, and finally everyone just flat-out refused. This kind of an exam was always degrading, and of course American soldiers were not used to being examined by a woman doctor. She finally gave up and went on her way.

All day long we could see quite a few American-made Russian fighters roaring around. Crazy, mad Europe! It had been two weeks now since we were "liberated," and I was beginning to wonder whether I would ever see the United States again.

About 5:00 A.M. on May 9, 1945, I was awakened by the chatter of machine guns, rifles, pistols, and anti-aircraft guns. Were the Germans counterattacking? Nothing I could do about it, I thought, and tried to go back to sleep. It finally dawned on me that the persistent rumors of the war's end must be true! The Russians were celebrating! Then a guy who had liberated a radio from a home in Riesa came around yelling that the war was over!

During the day the Russian soldiers were tearing all around in cars, trucks, motorcycles, and even a jeep, firing their guns in the air, and all very drunk. One drunken soldier passed out on the sidewalk in front of our building. They deserved the celebration. The soldiers and the whole Soviet Union had endured absolute hell for many years.

During the day some of us had cursory physical exams and initially it was thought I might have a hernia. It turned out my problem was just indigestion. Despite this I could tell I had put on a few pounds and definitely weighed more than the 120 to 125 pounds I had previously sunk to.

Later in the day, five American trucks arrived to take some of us back to the American lines, about twenty miles to the west. But the Russians refused to let any of us go, saying the plans for this were not fully completed. The Americans said they hoped to be back in two more days.

Two days later, on May 11, 1945, an American jeep showed up carrying a Russian-speaking American major from the

273rd Regiment of the Sixty-ninth Division and a representative of the American Red Cross. They explained they had twenty-five trucks on the road outside the camp and were going to start taking us back. The Red Cross man had also brought along a truck load of small drawstring cloth bags, compliments of the American Red Cross, containing toilet articles and some cigarettes for each former prisoner. Happy day!

Our mood changed quickly when Russian officers said they still had no approval to release us. The truck containing the release kits would be allowed in, but that was it. Then all the trucks would have to leave. I began to get a sinking feeling that something was very wrong.

When I finally got the chance, I spoke to the American Red Cross representative about my brother, Sergeant Robert Zak. He listened with great interest and took down his name and last-known unit number. Then he said when the situation finally got straightened out and he was allowed to return with the trucks, he would see if Bob could be in one of the trucks. Wow!

Things were looking up again! And now after all these many months, I even had a toothbrush. But after the Red Cross rep and the major left, time dragged very slowly. The next day—no trucks. The day after—no trucks.

But about 4:00 P.M., on May 14, three days after I met the man from the Red Cross, an American lieutenant came to the camp in a jeep, and as some of us gathered around him, he said he came to tell us for the last time that we better take off while the taking off was good, and told us to spread the word. He didn't offer any other explanation.

The lieutenant went on to say that his trucks would be on the road every day between Oschatz and the Mulde River to the west of Riesa. If we would be west of Oschatz between 11:00 A.M. and 1:00 P.M. we would be picked up. Oschatz was about ten miles west of our camp and the Mulde River was about twenty miles west.

Since it looked like we would rot there forever, or possibly even be shipped to Russia for all I knew, I decided to take up the lieutenant on his offer. I would head for Oschatz and beyond, and keep going west. Maybe some American trucks would be there, maybe not. At any rate my ultimate goal would be the town of Naunhof, west of Trebsen, which I had learned was the headquarters of the Sixty-ninth Division. There I would inquire about my brother.

I knew some guys had already left, and others were getting ready to go. But we all had the same problem. The Russians had posted some armed guards all around the camp and were turning back anyone they caught trying to leave. But I could see that some of the guards were not very diligent, and with a little luck, I should be able to get out.

I heard that one group tried three times to get out and were found out and turned back each time. Then they caught a glimpse of a guard hiding in some bushes to catch them. They sweated him out for a long time before he finally ambled farther down the line. Then they were up and away.

But how best to get out without being caught? I decided my best bet would be to try to leave about an hour before dawn through a vegetable garden at the end of the camp. I walked slowly over and through a gate to get the lay of the land during daylight hours and almost bumped into one of the Russian guards. He grabbed my left wrist on top of my watch, stared at me, and said, "Watch!" It seems the Russians had never seen wristwatches before and were crazy about them. He wanted my watch.

But I was fond of my cheap watch and had managed to hold on to it all this time through thick and thin. I impulsively reached over with my right hand and pushed up the loose-fitting sleeve on his right arm. He had at least six watches on his arm! I smiled at him and he smiled back, and let go of my wrist. He didn't make any more fuss. I guess he knew there were plenty more watches available among all these nice Yanks, and he would get plenty more before he was done. No doubt he was going to make a tidy profit selling them back in Russia.

So about an hour before dawn on the morning of May 15, 1945, five of us, including my friend Larkin Mayfield, climbed out a basement window and made our way in the dark through the vegetable garden. We jumped over a fence on the east side of the camp, the opposite direction from Oschatz, and headed south for about a half a mile or so to avoid the Russian guards. After walking west for a mile or two, we turned northwest to get on the road to Oschatz.

We soon came upon a large open farm field that was bordered by a long defensive German army trench we had to cross over. The trench looked unoccupied, but in the dim light of early morning, we couldn't be sure. And the whole area in front of the trenches could be filled with land mines.

Mindful of our training, I said, "Fellows, the field could be full of land mines. We better walk single file with about ten yards between each man." In the wink of an eye, everyone ran behind me, leaving me as the first guy in line. I had been the most observant. I was the smartest. Or was I? I swallowed hard and started off, recalling the motto of the infantry, "Follow Me." Reluctantly, I was now the leader. To everyone's relief, especially mine, we crossed the field without a problem.

As we swung onto the road to Oschatz, we saw a Russian soldier in a wagon drawn by two nice horses, heading in the direction we wanted to go. He had a load of milk cans. I called out to him and he stopped and let us climb aboard. We road along for about five kilometers until we left him at a fork in the road. In hopes he would forget he ever saw us, we each gave him some of our cigarettes.

We spent the rest of the day wandering along, stopping to explore abandoned homes, farms, and farmyards along the way, always looking for food or anything else of value to us. We never found anything. We did come upon a dead horse in a barnyard that had a large hunk of his upper rear leg cut off. Someone or some group had had a meal at the horse's expense.

Sometime during our wanderings during the day, three of the guys took off on their own, leaving Larkin Mayfield and me by ourselves. At one point Larkin and I were on the road doubling back east to take another look at a building that interested us. Suddenly we saw an armed German soldier walking on the road toward us, his rifle slung over his shoulder. He was trudging west, no doubt in hopes of escaping capture by the Russians. Did he recognize us as Americans? Would he consider us a threat? We pretended not to notice him, And he pretended not to notice us. We passed like two ships in the night. But I wouldn't bet a nickel he was going to slip past the Russians at the Mulde River.

Mayfield and I reached the outskirts of the town of Oschatz about 10:00 P.M. Just then a car pulled up with an Englishman at the wheel. The car had "USA" painted crudely on the back. He told us to hop in. He was wearing a G.I. uniform and a British garrison cap, and it turned out he had some of the German civilians believing he was an American army officer. It didn't make much sense to me. At any rate he spoke fluent German and had been very busy finding lodging for the night for the American and British ex-prisoners who were showing up.

He took us to a very beautiful, modern German home and spoke with forceful authority to the German woman who answered the door. He told her in German to see that we had supper and a bed for the night. It turned out the house was occupied by two women who were about thirty years of age or so and a man of about sixty years of age.

The women served us hamburger, ham, tea and margarine, and the man expertly cut slices of bread for us from a loaf that he held on his lap. They were very pleasant toward us, and Larkin and I felt very well fed and relaxed.

Larkin couldn't wait to try out the feather bed we were going to share, but I sat up for a while enjoying the rare civilized feminine company. Apparently they enjoyed my company as well. One of the women was quite charming and attractive, and far more wise in the ways of the world than I was at a mere nineteen years of age.

At any rate she wanted to tell me all about herself and her family. This was very difficult because I understood only some basic German. Fortunately, she knew a smattering of English. So she talked on, and tried to answer my questions, using pantomime when necessary. She was an "arteest," a dancer, and had worked in France, Peru, and Brazil before the war. Up to recently she had lived in Dresden, where both her parents and three small cousins had been killed in the massive bombing three months ago. Her brother was a prisoner of war somewhere in Russia and her husband was a P.O.W. in Canada. She and her family had paid dearly for Germany's monstrous aggression. I finally went to bed and fell into a deep sleep.

Two Brothers Meet near Oschatz, Germany

After a very early breakfast of bread, ersatz jam, and ersatz coffee, we thanked our hosts, said farewell, and started out for the Mulde River, about ten miles farther west. We probably would take two days to get there unless those American trucks showed up. But last night that fake American officer told us there weren't going to be any trucks. Apparently we all had been told that just to get us out of Russian control at Riesa. But we were happy to be on our way toward the American lines. It was May 16, 1945.

All morning long American-built Russian trucks and jeeps passed by from time to time in both directions, but no one bothered us.

We had walked about five miles when about 10:30 A.M. we saw two men in a jeep, with a two-wheel trailer, approaching from the west. At first we thought it was just another Russian jeep, but as it got closer, we saw this one was flying an American flag on the front! As it passed by, I was sure I recognized the driver as that American Red Cross rep! I couldn't see the face of his passenger. The jeep screeched to a halt and out jumped the Red Cross rep—and my brother Bob, looking fit as a fiddle! Praise the Lord! As we walked toward each other, he had a worried look on his face, but when he saw I looked okay, he broke out in a broad smile.

We shook hands, clapped each other on the shoulder, and looked with amazement and pleasure at each other. Our meeting pleased the American Red Cross representative to no end. He was smiling as happily as we were. Larkin Mayfield looked a little stunned at what had happened.

Our reunion moved to the side of the road where Bob assured me our parents were okay but had been out of their minds with worry about my health and whereabouts since December. Finally, on April 12, four months after my capture, they received the first of several brief letters from me that had been mailed in January. I found out later that the War Department did not confirm to my parents that I had been a prisoner of war until May 11, just five days before Bob and I met.

Good old Bob had brought along a box for me filled with the latest letters he had received from home as well as a bunch of candy bars, cigarettes, two cigars, peanuts, some magazines, and socks and underwear. What a guy!

But Bob and our Red Cross friend still had a job to finish. They had to go on to Riesa to deliver the trailer load of those small bags of toilet articles to the men who didn't get one the first time. It was quickly agreed that Larkin Mayfield and I would wait where we were and be picked up on their return trip. It would be a number of hours before they would be back.

So Larkin and I found a shady spot near the road where we started by eating a bunch of candy bars. Larkin, a real smoke eater if there ever was one, then smoked two cigars, one after the other.

Several hours later who should show up walking along the road but two of the other three guys we had started out with. I gave Mayfield three packs of the cigarettes and gave the rest to the other two guys. We all then settled down to wait to be picked up when the jeep returned. The others spent some of their time reading the magazines while I read all the letters from home. Life can be beautiful!

It was about 4:30 P.M. when Bob and our Red Cross friend arrived. (It irritates me to no end that years ago I lost my record of his name when I moved from one house to another.) The trailer was now empty of cloth bags but had a big load of G.I.s they had picked up along the road, and three or four more G.I.s were crammed in the back seat of the jeep. Several of them got off to make room for Mayfield and me, and we started off for the Mulde River and the town of Trebsen just across the bridge.

As we rode along, Bob described the tense, uneasy time they had when they arrived at the camp at Riesa with the release kits. They drove through the gate into the camp and Bob waited in the jeep while the Red Cross rep went into a building to see about distributing the kits.

While he waited, several ex-prisoners came up to him with letters they wanted him to take along. Soon others started throwing notes and letters from the windows of the building. Bob kept busy trying to collect them all. And at some point the release kits were unloaded from the trailer.

Finally, a determined-looking Russian soldier walked up, pointed his gun in Bob's face, and ordered him out of the camp. Having no choice, Bob drove out the gate and parked along the road to wait for the rep. These Russians are supposed to be our allies? Men were now throwing notes and letters to Bob over or through the fence, and Bob picked them all up.

Along the road came a Russian soldier on a motorcycle he had found somewhere. He zoomed by, weaving a little from side to side, then went off the road, smacked into a tree, and went flying through the air. Bob and the men looking out windows laughed and cheered at this little comic relief from all the tension everyone was under.

Then the Red Cross rep walked out the gate, and they took off. They found a number of American ex-prisoners waiting on the road for them and had them jump into the trailer and the back seat of the jeep. Away they went on the way to pick up Mayfield and me some fifteen miles or so down the road on the other side of Oschatz.

But as they rode along, they kept encountering G.I.s along the road. So Bob and the rep started a shuttle operation. They would drive a load of guys for a while, let them out, and go back for another load. Most of the time, Bob walked to make more room, and he helped some of the men who had trouble walking. The shuttle operation went on for hours and was a big help to many of the men trying to reach the American lines.

After they picked up Mayfield and me, the shuttle operation continued. Mayfield and I, as V.I.P.s, got to ride all the way. Finally, we arrived at a point not far from the river but outside the view of the Russians posted at the bridge. Scores of American ex-prisoners were gathered there, not attempting to proceed to the bridge.

The American Red Cross rep removed the American flag from the jeep and gave it to one of the G.I.s in the group. Then he told all the assembled men to follow the jeep to the bridge, walking behind the American flag. Would the Russians let us cross over? Bob insisted I wear his steel helmet and take his carbine. If the Russians were going to try to hold back all ex-prisoners, he hoped to pass me off as a soldier from the Sixty-ninth Infantry Division.

Dusk was coming on as we approached the bridge. The town of Trebsen and the American lines were on the other side. To our great relief, the Russians were off to one side and we crossed the bridge in our jeep to the American lines without any trouble. We were somewhat ahead of the men walking behind with the flag, and we planned to alert the American forces to send a rescue team if the Russians tried to stop them. But down the road they came, and crossed the bridge without interference, following the American flag! What a wonderful, glorious sight!

I was back! And in one piece! In short order we were greeted by soldiers who explained that we returnees would be taken by truck to a collection center at the city of Halle. I elected to stay with Bob, and said farewell to my friend Mayfield and the man from the American Red Cross.

It turned out that Bob was stationed right there in Trebsen, where he and his squad had taken over a private home. It had been empty except for a dead German soldier. Bob was part of the division signal company and was attached to the 273rd Regiment. His squad had a radio truck parked outside filled with all kinds of equipment, which was used to relay or send messages of all kinds.

Our next stop was the mess hall where we got some familiar G.I. chow, which tasted just great. All these months the only bread I ate came in dark, heavy two-kilo loaves made, it seemed, partially of sawdust. The G.I. white bread they had in the mess hall tasted like angel food cake.

Back at his "home," Bob introduced me to his squad and then told me how he found out I was in the area. He had been called to regimental headquarters and was introduced to the representative from the American Red Cross, who had just returned from his encounter with me. The rep had his jeep trailer loaded with more toilet kits and planned to go back to Riesa the next day. When the rep mentioned to Bob that he might want to come along, Bob told him very forcefully that he definitely was going.

But when they tried to cross the bridge the next day, the Russians stopped them and would not let them pass. The rep and the colonel discussed the situation and decided it would be best to wait a few days before trying again.

So every day Bob stood at the bridge waiting for stray Americans coming across the bridge, asking them if they knew me or had seen me. No such luck.

Finally, on the morning of May 16, 1945, they decided to try again. This time they brought along an interpreter and cartons of cigarettes. The Russians wouldn't budge. So the interpreter went back and got more cartons of cigarettes, and this time the guards agreed. But they told them to avoid driving near their lieutenant. So the interpreter waved them on, and off they went. Just hours later, we met.

During the evening Bob and I caught up on our lives and what was going on back on the home front. He explained his outfit was in England when the Battle of the Bulge started, and they were rushed over as soon as possible. Bob's outfit fought all the way to the Mulde River here in Germany, where by agreement between the American and Russian high commands, the American advance, except for patrols, was to stop. One of Bob's many stories was about the time his radio truck coordinated all the orders for the bombardment of a huge monument in Leipzig where diehard German troops were holding out inside.

Finally, Bob and I wrote a joint letter to our mother and dad, telling them of our joyful meeting and assuring them that we were both safe, well, and happy.

It was agreed that for my health's sake I should go on to the official collecting point. So the following morning, after a good breakfast, Bob and I, along with his section sergeant, started out by jeep. On the way we passed through the city of Leipzig.

The city of Leipzig was a mess, a total wreck. Many buildings were now just rubble, and I saw a few abandoned German weapons scattered here and there. Bombs and artillery had done their work. The huge monument was all full of holes and scars made by the artillery bombardment Bob had talked about. And I could see groups of German civilians passing bricks down a long human train to a wagon at the base of a mountain of rubble a block square. It all seemed so bizarre and futile. And this was the city I would have been sent to on a work party if I hadn't slipped away from that formation back at Stalag IV-B. It was a smart move.

Back in the U.S. Army

We finally arrived at the city of Halle, Germany, where the U.S. Army had set up a center to collect ex-prisoners, including British soldiers or airmen. The three of us enjoyed a meal together, and then Bob and his section sergeant left. Bob said he would be in touch.

I signed in and was given forms to fill out identifying myself and so forth. I was now an official "R.A.M.P.," part of a group designated "Recovered Allied Military Personnel." It was May 17, 1945. They also had me fill in a form so they could send a briefly worded, stock telegram to my parents stating I had returned to U.S. Army military control. That was a very happy, satisfying moment. I was assigned a cot and I was all set.

Later, I had an opportunity to weigh myself. I now weighed 132 pounds, up from my estimated 120 to 125 low, but far below the 155 pounds I had weighed before my capture.

I had a lot of leisure time, and I spent a lot of it searching for old friends. I never saw a single one while I was there, not even Larkin Mayfield. So I mostly moped around, waiting for something to happen.

On my second day back, I woke up with an upset stomach and my eyes were killing me. I guess I was having trouble getting used to normal food, three times a day. I, of course skipped breakfast, and by about noon, my only problem was a headache.

My headache vanished when Bob and his section sergeant walked in. They had made the trip all the way from Trebsen to see me. They had a camera and we drove over to a nearby military airfield and took some pictures of Bob and me and also had someone take a picture of the three of us. The backdrop of some of the pictures were German fighter planes parked around the field. Bob said he would have the film developed and send the pictures to our folks along with the letter we had written. The day had started out so rotten and ended so wonderfully.

This would be our final visit together. I was expecting to be shipped to France very soon and Bob had to get back to supervising his radio team. We said our last good-byes and I promised if I got home before he did, I would tell Dad and Mom how great he looked.

Five days after I had arrived, I finally got word that my assigned group of twenty-five would be leaving today. Late in the afternoon, we were loaded on trucks, and twenty minutes later, we arrived in a light drizzle at a large airport. Wrecked German planes were everywhere, including some pick-a-back Heinkels. And dozens of American C-47 cargo planes stretched in long lines. We drove right up to one and were put aboard without delay.

Fold-down bench seats lined both sides, and we were up and away about 6:30 P.M. After take-off, instead of sitting, I stood most of the way behind the pilot, fascinated by the whole experience. I had never flown in a two-engine plane before. The only time I had been in a plane was a short ride in a small, open-cockpit, two-seater when I was about sixteen years old.

The young pilot was very relaxed and was happy to answer all my questions and show me points of interest. For the first forty-five minutes, we flew at an altitude of only about 800 feet, at a speed of 165 miles per hour. What a view! Then we climbed to about 3,000 feet and stayed there. Along the way I got a good look at the old German Seigfried Line and the Ardennes Forest. We passed from Germany to Luxembourg, and about fifteen minutes later, we entered France. Just before

105

9:00 P.M. our wheels touched down at Rheims. Viva La France!

We were taken by truck to an army base and had a good meal. The next morning we all got showers, delousing, a typhus shot, and a new uniform. Our beat-out old ones were all to be burned. I was starting to feel more like a soldier again.

Late that afternoon we boarded a train and passed through cities such as Laon and Ham. This is really the land of the poppies. They are all over. This is part of where World War I was fought. It brought back a rush of memories of my father's rough times in the combat engineers in this area twenty-seven years earlier.

After leaving the train for a meal, we reboarded and passed through Amiens. I couldn't sleep; the train was icy cold. When we stopped again in the middle of the night for another meal, I, along with two lieutenants who had also been prisoners of war, went looking for blankets. We found a supply tent, but the sergeant wouldn't let us have any blankets. We decided to slip back after the meal and help ourselves, but the supply sergeant beat us back. So that was that.

Finally, about 9:00 A.M., we pulled into the train station at St. Vallery, France. St. Vallery? My dad had been stationed here in 1919 after World War I ended. I hoped if I ever had any sons they wouldn't end up over there in World War III.

We were loaded on trucks again, and finally arrived at a huge tent city known as "Camp Lucky Strike." The entire camp was filled with American ex-prisoners of war from both the ground and air forces. It was used as a staging area before being loaded on ships bound for the States. I couldn't wait.

The next day I ran into guys from the company I had first served in when I arrived at the 106th Infantry Division, Company D. The group included John Wilson, Sigmund Tergeson, and Charlie Self. We caught up on what happened to each other and what we had heard about others. One of the guys shocked me when he said he had heard a good buddy of mine,

Staff Sergeant Charlie Smith, had been killed. (After I got home, I found out he had been captured but survived in fair shape.)

I spent the days from May 24, when I arrived, to June 9 searching for friends and going for meals. My digestion problems seemed to be over. I got weighed on June 1 and weighed 143 pounds. I had gained weight, but it was mostly on my belly. Not much muscle. I was not the healthy, strong, 155-pound soldier I once had been. In contrast, I stood in line each afternoon for a cup of eggnog served by tanned, healthy German prisoners. Who said life was supposed to be fair?

The S.S. *Excelsior* and Home

On the morning of June 9, 1945, a large group of us arrived at the devastated city of Le Havre and were driven to the docks. Wrecked cranes and other damaged harbor equipment were all in plain view. We boarded a cargo ship, which had been converted into a troop carrier. I thought it was a Liberty Ship, but I wasn't sure. Its name was the S.S. *Excelsior,* manned by an American crew.

As we filed onto the deck, we were lined up for a final inspection. A medic looked in my eyes and said I had jaundice. He said the whites of my eyes were somewhat yellow, which I knew, and he said I would have to leave the ship! I was shocked. I wanted to go home, real bad. I told him I felt just fine, and it would probably clear up by the time we got to the States. He bought it, or just felt sorry for me, and let me stay on board.

That evening the ship finally pulled away from the dock, and an hour later we stopped to let off the harbor pilot. Now we were really on our way! As I took a last look at France, I thought about all the dead American soldiers and airmen we were leaving behind. And I felt bad that I was heading home while my brother Bob was still somewhere in Germany.

For the first few days, I didn't feel so hot and stayed in my bunk a lot. It was kind of eerie because the steel plates on the side groaned as if they were going to pull loose. I finally got my sea legs and spent a lot of time on deck. Food was plentiful, good old American-type, and I was pleased that our trip was about half over. The June weather was pleasant and all was well in our little part of the world.

The only unpleasant part was the music played over the P.A. system. The guy in charge, whoever he was, was crazy about a popular song and played it almost all the time, every day. After the first forty or fifty times it was starting to drive me nuts. It was called "Rum and Coca-Cola," recorded by the Andrews Sisters. The lyrics were about a mother and a daughter working for the Yankee dollar.

One day we heard that our ship was changing course. Instead of going to New York, we were now heading for Hampton Roads and Newport News, near Norfolk, Virginia. I was a little disappointed because I had missed seeing the Statue of Liberty on our way to Scotland and now I was going to miss it again.

The last few nights, I slept on deck with a lot of others because it was too hot and stuffy below deck. Late at night on June 17, we passed about six buoys with white blinking lights and later I could see a faint glow in the sky on the horizon. Millions of stars were out and I could tell by the Big Dipper and the North Star that we were heading due west.

As our ship tied up at the dock the next morning, I didn't hear a sound from those around me. Most of us stood at the rails, lost in our own thoughts, as we looked absentmindedly at the small military band playing on the dock. All of us on board were ex-prisoners of war, and had not come home as victorious heroes. Many of us, maybe all, had some feelings of guilt about surviving as prisoners of war while so many others had died on some battlefield.

A short time later, we were escorted off the ship and taken directly to a nearby mess hall. We went happily through the chow line and filled our trays as much as possible. Eating a good meal was still a novelty to us.

We all ate as quickly as possible and got back in the chow line for "seconds." One of the young recruits dishing out the food was amazed at our voracious appetites and said, "Hey, didn't they feed you guys over there?" Too busy getting more food, no one bothered to answer.

I was home! I had survived! But had I been brave enough, I wondered? Had I done my duty? I know I never disobeyed an order, including the one to "Advance!" at Schonberg. What would others think? Those questions haunted me off and on for years.

Epilogue

And what became of the American and British prisoners I had left behind at Riesa? The best source of information I have about this is the book *Soldiers of Misfortune* published in 1992 by National Press Books, Inc., Washington, D.C., written by Sanders, Sauter, and Kirkwood.

According to their well-documented book, the Soviets held our men until May 25, ten days after I had slipped away. On this date most of these men were formally exchanged for Russian prisoners brought to the camp by American forces. The authors quote by name an American prisoner who saw the Russian prisoners marched off to a nearby quarry where they were all machine-gunned to death. A personal ex-prisoner friend of mine tells the same story.

American and British prisoners had been imprisoned by the German army in scores of prison camps scattered all over Germany. Others were held in camps in East Prussia, Poland, Austria, and other locations. As the Russian army advanced into Poland and then into Germany, the Russians took control over large numbers of American and British prisoners.

All my suspicions and great fears about the Russians seem to have been confirmed by the authors of this book. They spell out very shocking and convincing evidence that, of the 78,000 Americans who were never found after World War II, thousands were American prisoners of the Germans who were shipped by the Russians to prison camps in the vast gulag system in the Soviet Union. The authors also contend that the Russians imprisoned thousands of British ex-prisoners of the

Germans. All the rest of the men who had been captured by the Germans eventually made it back to Allied lines.

Why would the Russians have done such a horrible thing? The authors provide compelling evidence that these men were kept by the Soviets as hostages or bargaining chips because they found out that the U.S. and British governments had not kept agreements made at Yalta in the Soviet Union and at Halle, Germany, to return all Soviet nationals under their control. They wanted them all back.

The American and British governments were caught in a very bad bind. They had secretly hidden away many Soviets who were anti-Communists and who had fought against the Soviets as members of the German army. Prime Minister Churchill of England, and many others, feared the Soviets saw the Cold War beginning, and felt a desperate need to recruit many secret agents who could help find out the real intentions of the Soviet government. Again, according to the authors, the American and British governments were convinced that they absolutely had to have those agents.

They also realized that if they did not return these Soviet nationals, and took military action to try to rescue the hostages, a monumental war with the Soviets was certain to follow. Again, according to the authors of *Soldiers of Misfortune,* top government officials secretly made the painful, ghastly decision that these men would have to be sacrificed as casualties of the Cold War to save the lives of untold others, possibly millions, if a war broke out. Very few of these men ever returned. All records were altered to hide this monstrous tragedy.

I would add that everyone skeptical about the possibility of such a nightmare should read this book and all the very, very convincing documentation. I desperately want to believe the authors of *Soldiers of Misfortune* are wrong, wrong, wrong, but their proof seems overwhelming.

Additional corroboration that thousands of American soldiers disappeared while in Soviet hands was discussed in an article in *The Wall Street Journal* on July 19, 1989, authored by Bill Paul. The article was captioned "Will Gorbachev Find World War II's Long-Lost POWs?" Mr. Paul reported that more than 5,000 American soldiers who had been prisoners of the Germans were still missing nine months after the war had ended! At that same point in time only eighty-six Americans captured by the Japanese were still missing.

My heart bleeds every time I think about the overwhelming evidence that young Americans just like myself were sacrificed as the first casualties of the Cold War between Russia and the Western nations. What could their lives have been like, and how must they have felt about being abandoned by their own country?

In my own case, after I returned to the United States, I was sent on a two-month recuperation leave, to be assigned to another infantry unit after I returned. Japan still had to be invaded and conquered.

Before I left I was awarded the Combat Infantry Badge, the Bronze Star Medal, and Battle Stars for the Ardennes, Rhineland, and Central Europe Campaigns. I turned down the Purple Heart Medal they said I was entitled to for my now-healed frozen feet. I would have been embarrassed to explain why I got it when other men had been awarded this medal because they had lost an eye or an arm or a leg.

Just before I was due to report back for active duty, two atomic bombs were dropped on Japanese cities in the hope this would bring about the end of the war. But the Japanese High Command was divided. Some wanted to surrender, but others wanted to defend the Japanese homeland with a fanatical, all-out blood bath, starting with the slaughter of all remaining Allied prisoners of war. Emperor Hirohito finally sided with those who wanted to end the war. He issued a decree by radio to the nation, and the military and civilian population, who worshiped Hirohito as a living god, dutifully followed his order to surrender.

When I returned to active duty, I was promoted to the rank of corporal and assigned to an infantry unit at Camp Blanding, Florida. But since there no longer was a war to fight, I was assigned to typing reports concerning men who had applied for a dependency discharge from the army.

Finally, on December 3, 1945, three months after my twentieth birthday, and two years after I entered the army, I was given an honorable discharge from military service.

A month or so later, I became a freshman at a local (Chicago) university with my tuition paid by our government's G.I. Bill. It was quite a shock to switch mental gears and focus on my new life situation. Just months previously I had ended a six-month nightmare and now had to forget all that and concentrate on my studies.

Of course most of the young men in college with me had been in military service, but few I met had had any combat experience. The women students were younger and wonderful to be around, but most seemed so infantile and immature.

As I look back on those days, I now realize I was still immature myself, and kind of neurotic as well. I told only a few male friends about my wartime experiences, and only in a brief, general way. I held all my horrible memories to myself, for reasons I did not then understand.

I only really understood why I had such problems in those days when I read the book *Healing the Child Warrior*, published in 1992 by Consultors Incorporated, Cardiff by the Sea, California, written by Richard Peterson. I had never met him, but he also had been a prisoner of war. It is a scholarly but very readable explanation of the mental dynamics of being a prisoner of war.

Despite my personal problems, I was determined to make

something of myself and became a serious, dedicated student. I did very well academically and completed my bachelor's degree with honors. I then got a job, and several years later completed a master's degree.

Eight years after the war, I married the girl of my dreams, Joan McAndrew. Besides our love, we shared a special bond. Her brother, Harold McAndrew, had been taken prisoner by the Japanese on Bataan in the Philippines. He survived the Bataan Death March only to die months later of abuse and starvation.

Over the years Joan and I raised and educated three fine young men and a beautiful young lady, and now have three wonderful grandchildren. After several years doing psychological testing I went on to a fairly successful business career and spent most of my leisure time with my family or on church committee work. And once a year, about thirty local-area survivors of the war and Stalag IV-B get together to celebrate life and remember our friends and other comrades who didn't make it home again. I must add that I am truly grateful to my Creator that I survived the war and went on to a meaningful, satisfying, productive life.

I have been reflecting all these years on all I had experienced as a very young man during World War II, and I knew that one day I had to put it all down on paper. And now, finally, I did. My war is over.